NICARAGUA
in Pictures

Christopher Dall

TF
CB
Twenty-First Century Books

Contents

Website address: www.lernerbooks.com

Twenty-First Century Books
A division of Lerner Publishing Group
241 First Avenue North
Minneapolis, MN 55401 U.S.A.

web enhanced @ www.vgsbooks.com

CULTURAL LIFE　48

▶ Language and Literature. Music. Film, Theater, and Media. Art and Architecture. Religion. Holidays and Festivals. Sports. Food.

THE ECONOMY　58

▶ Agriculture. Manufacturing. Services and Tourism. Energy and Mining. Foreign Trade. Transportation. The Future.

FOR MORE INFORMATION

Library of Congress Cataloging-in-Publication Data

Dall, Christopher.
　　Nicaragua in pictures / by Christopher Dall.
　　　　p.　cm. — (Visual geography series)—Rev. & expanded.
　　Includes bibliographical references and index.
　　ISBN-13: 978-0-8225-2671-1 (lib. bdg. : alk. paper)
　　ISBN-10: 0-8225-2671-9 (lib. bdg. : alk. paper)
　　1 Nicaragua. 2. Nicaragua—Pictorial works. I. Title. II. Series: Visual geography series (Minneapolis, Minn.)
　F1523.D35 2007
　972.85'0022'2—dc22
　　　　　　　　　　　　　　　　　　　　　　　　　　　　　　2005005757

Manufactured in the United States of America
1 2 3 4 5 6 - BP - 12 11 10 09 08 07

INTRODUCTION

The Republic of Nicaragua is a country located in Central America. It sits at the elbow of the Central American isthmus—a piece of land between the Pacific and Atlantic oceans that stretches southward from Mexico to South America. It is a land of great beauty and friendly people. But it is also a nation that has been scarred by natural disasters and by conflict. In recent years, however, Nicaragua has finally begun to emerge from its difficult past, giving the Nicaraguan people hope for a more prosperous future.

People have lived in Nicaragua for thousands of years. The original inhabitants were indigenous (native) peoples who survived by hunting and gathering. Later, Nicaragua became home to people who migrated from Mexico and South America. In the 1500s, explorers and settlers from Spain arrived and Nicaragua became a Spanish colony. Spanish settlers brought their language, customs, and religion with them. The intermarriage of white Spanish settlers with indigenous people produced children known as mestizos—people of mixed

heritage. Europeans also brought Africans to Central America to work as slaves. They settled primarily along the Caribbean coast.

Nicaragua is known for its stunning landscapes, including fertile farmland, numerous volcanoes, and vast rain forests. But its history has been marked by poverty, hardship, and political violence. Nicaragua has been an underdeveloped nation for much of its modern history, burdened by political instability and corrupt leadership. Constant political turmoil and ongoing poverty throughout the nineteenth and twentieth centuries have led Nicaragua to be viewed as Central America's most troubled nation. More than ten thousand people died in its most recent conflict, a civil war fought during the 1980s.

Since the early 1990s, Nicaraguans have been working hard to rebuild a nation shattered by warfare. But although their country is at peace, they have had to deal with economic problems such as high inflation (rising prices), unemployment, and high foreign debt. These problems have made Nicaragua the second-poorest nation in the

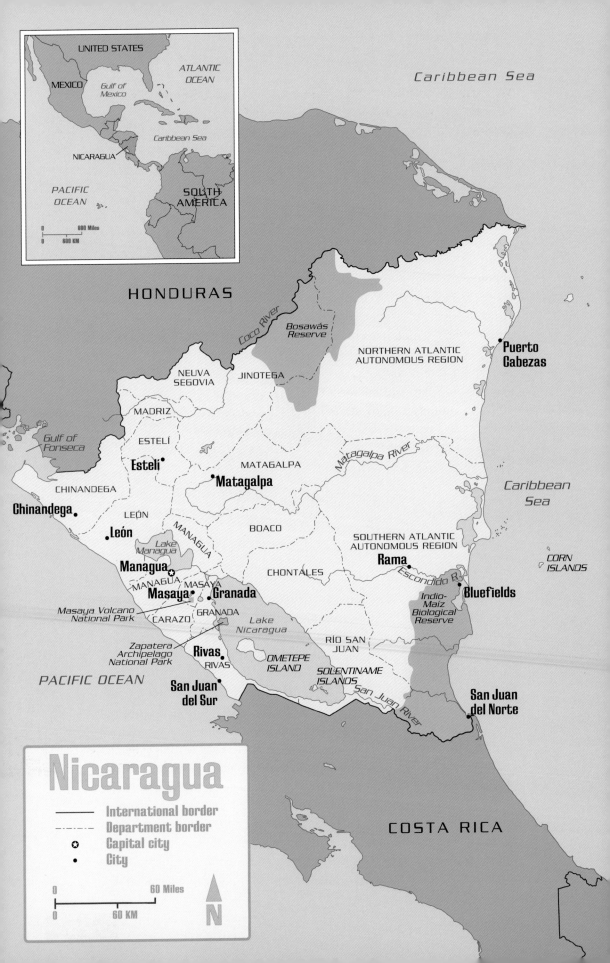

Western Hemisphere. Many rural Nicaraguans live in extreme poverty. They have little access to adequate health care. The country is also faced with environmental problems, including the destruction of its forests.

Nevertheless, Nicaragua is making progress as it tries to distance itself from its painful past. Although it is still primarily an agricultural nation that relies on heavily on the export of coffee beans, it is slowly becoming more industrialized. Government reforms have led to better economic performance, which has encouraged foreign nations to invest in Nicaragua. The country is also trying to promote its natural beauty—its lush forests, unspoiled beaches, and volcanic mountains—to attract tourists and create a more inviting image. Nicaraguans are hopeful that their country is headed in the right direction and that continued political stability and increased foreign investment will help make their country strong, peaceful, and vibrant.

The name *Nicaragua* is a combination of *Nicarao*, which was the largest tribe in the region when the Spanish conquistadors arrived, and the Spanish word *agua* (water), which referred to the two large lakes along the country's Pacific coast.

THE LAND

Nicaragua is the largest country in Central America. Roughly trian-
gular in shape and with 50,193 square miles of territory (130,000
square kilometers), it is slightly larger than New York State. The
Pacific Ocean lies to the west of Nicaragua, while the Caribbean Sea
is to the east. In the north, rugged mountains form much of the border with Honduras. In the south, the San Juan River separates
Nicaragua from Costa Rica.

Nicaragua is almost at the center point between North and
South America. It sits at the only large break in a long chain of
mountains running along the Pacific coast from Alaska to the
 southern tip of South America. Geologically, Nicaragua separates
North America from the southern portion of Central America, where
the mountains rise again to continue their march down the South
American continent.

Nicaragua is home to a great variety of landscapes and to several
ecosystems. Its most outstanding features are its volcanic mountains

and its large lakes. In fact, Nicaragua's nickname is the Land of Lakes and Volcanoes. But the country also boasts fertile farmland and vast tropical rain forests. The most populated of the nation's three regions is the Pacific Lowlands. This area contains Nicaragua's major cities and is an important agricultural region. The more sparsely populated Central Highlands produces much of the country's largest export— coffee. The Caribbean Lowlands is the least populated area of Nicaragua. It holds rich tropical rain forests and a wide array of plant and animal species.

▶ The Pacific Lowlands

Most of Nicaragua's people live in the Pacific Lowlands. This strip of land is about 40 miles (64 km) wide and extends along the Pacific coast from Honduras to Costa Rica. The mostly rolling lowlands rise as high as 3,000 feet (914 meters) above sea level. The bulk of Nicaragua's agricultural output comes from this fertile area. Crops include rice, corn, beans, bananas, beef, and dairy products. The harvests of the region are taken to markets in major cities such as Managua, León, Granada, and Chinandega.

In the southern and western part of the country lie Nicaragua's two great lakes—Lake Nicaragua and Lake Managua. Lake Managua is a 38-mile-long (61 km) body of water that drains into Lake Nicaragua from the northwest. Lake Nicaragua measures 100 miles (161 km) long and 45 miles (72 km) wide. It is considered one of the country's greatest national treasures. The San Juan River flows out of Lake Nicaragua and travels east to the Caribbean Sea.

Nicaragua lies in a region of intense volcanic activity. Nearly forty volcanoes dot the Pacific region from north to south. Six of them remain active and occasionally send out plumes of smoke and gas, and even streams of lava. Cosigüina Volcano, overlooking the Gulf of Fonseca, on Nicaragua's northwestern border, is one of the nation's most impressive peaks. It was formed 150 years ago in an explosion that sent clouds of ash as far east as the island of Jamaica.

A chain of volcanoes forms the eastern border of the Pacific Lowlands. Among the most active in this chain are Momotombo, San Cristóbal, and Telica. The most continually active volcano in Nicaragua is Masaya, just west of the city of Granada. While these volcanoes can cause destruction, they have also helped the country by depositing rich nutrients into the soil. These nutrients help make the farmland of the Pacific Lowlands especially fertile.

The same geologic forces that created Nicaragua's volcanoes are also responsible for the earthquakes that pose a constant threat. Nicaragua's

MOUNTAINS OF FIRE

Among Nicaragua's active volcanoes are Masaya, Concepción, Cerro Negro, Momotombo, San Cristóbal, and Telica. Active means the volcano has erupted within the past few hundred years, frequently emits gases, or is showing signs that it might soon erupt. The most recent volcanic activity in Nicaragua was in 2003, when the Masaya Volcano sent a cloud of gas and steam nearly 3 miles (4.8 km) into the air. Concepción, Nicaragua's highest and most active volcano, has erupted more than 25 times in the last 125 years. Cerro Negro is Central America's youngest volcano. Since its birth in 1850, it has grown more than 1,300 feet (396 m). Cerro Negro's 1992 eruption covered the city of León in a thick layer of dust and ash, causing several roofs to collapse. And although Momotombo hasn't erupted since 1905, some rumbling heard in the early 2000s caused great concern among the residents of Managua.

Momotombo Volcano appears to rise from Lake Managua in this photograph taken from Nicaragua's capital city, Managua.

largest cities are located near the volcanic zone, along a rift where the earth's crust is fragile and shifting. The capital city of Managua was shattered by an earthquake and fire in 1931, and it is still recovering from a 1972 earthquake that destroyed most of its central business district.

The Central Highlands

To the east of the chain of volcanic mountains lie the Central Highlands. The rolling highland terrain in this part of Nicaragua rises 2,000 to 5,000 feet (610 to 1,524 m) above sea level. It is dominated by three mountain ranges—the Isabella, Dariense, and Chontalena ranges. The highest peak in this region and in the nation is Mount Mogoton. Located on the Honduran border, it reaches an elevation of 8,000 feet (2,438 m). Between the forest-covered mountains, valleys point like long fingers toward the Caribbean Sea. Farming settlements and towns dot these valleys. The higher elevations of the north are home to the coffee plantations that produce Nicaragua's most valuable crop. To the south, small farming operations produce daily staples such as corn, rice, and red beans.

The Caribbean Lowlands

The mountains of Nicaragua's central region melt into hot, humid tropical lowlands in the eastern part of the country. The Caribbean Lowlands make up nearly one-third of Nicaragua. They have been nicknamed the Mosquito Coast after the disease-carrying insect that once spread fever among the inhabitants. These lowlands extend along the Caribbean Sea in a band nearly 100 miles (161 km) wide in the north near the Honduran border and about 50 miles (80 km) wide along the Costa Rican frontier. The region is made up of lush tropical rain forests, mangrove islands, murky rivers, and inhospitable swamps. Most roads are unpaved.

Two major waterways help drain this region. The Coco River—Central America's longest—forms more than half the border with Honduras before emptying into the Caribbean Sea. The San Juan River in the south forms much of the border with Costa Rica. Several smaller rivers, including the Escondido, provide drainage in areas of heavy rainfall.

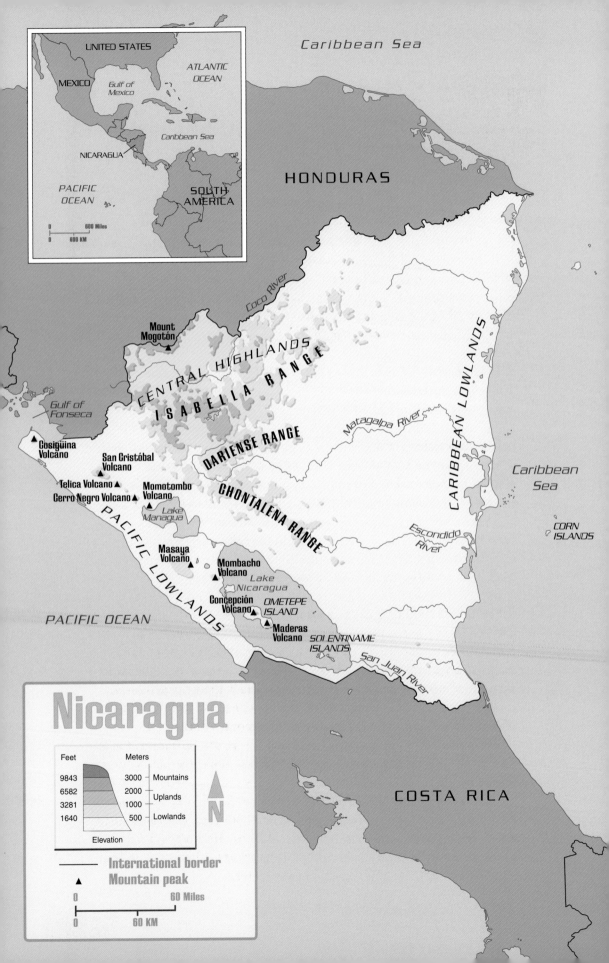

Caribbean Sea

HONDURAS

Coco River

Mount
Mogotón ▲

CENTRAL HIGHLANDS

ISABELLA RANGE

Gulf of
Fonseca

Cosigüina
Volcano ▲

San Cristóbal
Volcano ▲

DARIENSE RANGE

Matagalpa River

CARIBBEAN LOWLANDS

Telica Volcano ▲

Momotombo
Volcano ▲

Cerro Negro Volcano ▲

CHONTALENA RANGE

Lake
Managua

Caribbean
Sea

CORN
ISLANDS

PACIFIC LOWLANDS

Masaya
Volcano ▲

Escondido
River

Mombacho
Volcano ▲

Lake
Nicaragua

PACIFIC OCEAN

Concepción
Volcano ▲

OMETEPE
ISLAND

Maderas
Volcano ▲

SOLENTINAME
ISLANDS

San Juan River

COSTA RICA

Nicaragua

Feet	Meters	
9843	3000	Mountains
6582	2000	Uplands
3281	1000	Lowlands
1640	500	

Elevation

N

——— International border
▲ Mountain peak

0   60 Miles
0   60 KM

The largest coral reef system near **Big Corn Island** is the Cana Reef. It extends 1.3 miles (2 km) seaward from the northeast shore of Big Corn Island, and it is 2.5 miles (4 km) wide from northwest to southeast.

Nicaragua also owns several small islands along the Caribbean coast. The best known are the Corn Islands (Big Corn Island and Little Corn Island). These popular vacation resorts were once the haunts of pirates on their way to attack Spanish settlements along the Central American coast.

Climate

Nicaragua is in the tropics, a zone near the equator. Like other tropical regions, it enjoys warm temperatures all year-round. Nicaragua's climate is heavily influenced by warm winds that blow inland from both coasts. The nation's major areas of settlement are typically tropical—warm in the morning and afternoon, hot and humid at noon, and cooler at night. The highland areas of northwestern Nicaragua are noticeably cooler than the rest of the nation. Average temperatures there range from 60°F to 70°F (16°C to 21°C), compared to 85°F to 96°F (29°C to 36°C) in most of Nicaragua. April and May are the hottest months of the year.

Nicaragua has two major seasons. The rainy season lasts from May to October, while the dry season begins in about November and ends in April. Rainfall varies substantially throughout the country, with the rainy season lasting longer in the Caribbean Lowlands. The Pacific region sees about 60 inches (152 centimeters) per year, compared to up to 100 inches (254 cm) in the Central Highlands. Meanwhile, rainfall in the Caribbean Lowlands ranges from 165 inches (419 cm) annually in the north to 250 inches (635 cm) in the south.

Flora and Fauna

Nicaragua is rich in plant and animal life. The lush tropical rain forests covering the nation's eastern one-third of Nicaragua boast great natural diversity. Giant trees standing more than 100 feet (30 m) in height—with trunks that are 4 to 5 feet (1.2 to 1.5 m) in diameter—are common. They provide a leafy canopy for the many smaller plants that cover the forest floor. Extensive grasslands, with scattered stands of pine trees, lie among swampy areas of the coast. Forests of coconut palms line the Caribbean seashore.

Pine forests can be found in the northern part of Nicaragua's Central Highlands. Sizable forests in this region also produce valuable hardwoods, including mahogany. The Pacific Lowlands is home to dry grasslands and cactuslike plants. The volcanic mountains that border the Pacific Lowlands are covered in clouds for much of the year. The moist air provided by that cloud cover feeds cloud forests of ferns, moss, and a great variety of broad-leaved trees.

At least 176 species of mammals inhabit Nicaragua. More than half of these species are bats and small rodents, but the list also includes carnivorous (meat-eating) cats such as jaguars, pumas, and ocelots. The slopes of the Mombacho and Maderas volcanoes are home to the mantled howler monkey. Other small monkeys, including spider monkeys and capuchin monkeys, can be found in the Caribbean Lowlands. Among the other interesting creatures in Nicaragua are armadillos and anteaters, as well as peccaries (small mammals that are related to pigs).

Lake Nicaragua and the San Juan River are home to the bull shark, the only shark that can live in freshwater. Scientists have different theories about the shark's origins. Lake Nicaragua and Lake Managua were probably connected to the Pacific Ocean in prehistoric times. As a result, scientists originally believed the shark was an ancient species that was trapped when the land shifted and cut the lakes off from the ocean. Recent theories, however, suggest the sharks come from the Caribbean Sea and adjust for the change in the water's salinity (saltiness) as they travel up the San Juan River to the lake.

Nicaragua also boasts a wide variety of aquatic life. Coastal and inland waters contain fish, freshwater sharks, dolphins, and shellfish. Among the numerous reptiles are crocodiles that lurk in lowland waters and marine turtles that nest on both the Pacific and Caribbean coasts. Long boa constrictors live in the murky rivers of the Caribbean Lowlands. Poisonous serpents, including coral snakes and pit vipers, also thrive there. At least fifty-eight different types of marine coral have been identified along the Caribbean coast.

Nicaragua's bird life is varied, as well, with winged visitors arriving from both North and South America. Chickadees, swallows, mockingbirds, orioles, blackbirds, and jays compete for territory with bright-plumed macaws. Quail and ducks are found in the countryside, where hawks, ospreys, and falcons prey on smaller birds and rodents. Along the seashore, large wading birds—including herons and ibis—preen their feathers, while gulls, terns, pelicans, and cormorants patrol overhead on the lookout for something to eat in the water down below.

◉ Environmental Problems

The biggest environmental problem facing Nicaragua is deforestation—the destruction of its forests. A number of factors are responsible for deforestation. They include logging by foreign timber companies, population growth, the conversion of forest into farmland, and the use of wood for fuel. All of these forces are putting increasing pressure on Nicaragua's forests. Nicaragua has lost nearly

The Great Kiskadee is a songbird native to dry forests near Managua. Its song lasts just three seconds but may include more than twenty notes.

half of its forest cover since 1950. Some environmental groups believe the country could lose its forests completely within the next ten to fifteen years.

One of the major results of deforestation is soil erosion. In this process, rain washes away topsoil, because there are no tree roots left to hold the soil in place. Rain washes the topsoil into streams and rivers, clogging them and hurting the plants, animals, and fish that live there. The problem of deforestation and soil erosion was highlighted by Hurricane Mitch, which hit Nicaragua in 1998, and again by Hurricane Keith in 2000. These storms caused devastating mudslides in areas that had been deforested.

To fight deforestation and erosion, Nicaragua's government and environmental groups are trying to create new forests. They have begun planting young trees in deforested areas. They are also trying to teach Nicaraguan farmers to use less destructive farming methods. Because Nicaragua's population is growing and more people will need farmland and wood for fuel, these efforts will be crucial to the future of the country's forests.

Nicaragua has also experienced environmental problems associated with urban growth. Among these problems is air pollution, caused by factories and automobiles. But perhaps the greatest symbol of Nicaragua's environmental problems is the condition of Lake Managua. This lake is considered biologically dead after years of

On September 28, 2000, heavy rain from Hurricane Keith caused flooding and mudslides. The flooding, which killed twelve people in Nicaragua, forced this mother and child to flee their home 112 miles (180 km) northeast of Managua.

having human and industrial waste dumped into its waters. However, the international community is helping to pay for the construction of water treatment facilities to clean the lake.

Like its neighbor to the south, Costa Rica, Nicaragua has made efforts to preserve some of its natural beauty. The nation has created protected areas including national parks, biological reserves, and wildlife refuges. Among the most prominent are the Masaya Volcano National Park, the Indio Maíz Biological Reserve, and the Bosawas Reserve. But it is often difficult for the government to protect these areas. Many of the people who live in and around these regions are poor, and they need the land and its resources to survive.

Cities

Nicaragua's population is split between urban and rural areas, with nearly 60 percent of the population living in cities and 40 percent in the countryside. The nation's main cities are Managua, León, Chinandega, Masaya, and Granada.

MANAGUA With a population of 1,159,000, Managua is Nicaragua's capital, chief commercial center, and largest city. It is also the second-largest city in Central America. Managua was founded in the 1850s on the southern shore of Lake Managua. It is a bustling and chaotic city filled with outdoor marketplaces, museums, restaurants, and nightclubs.

Managua's central business district was destroyed by the 1972 earthquake, and the city still lacks a true downtown. The few remaining structures in the half-empty downtown area around the Plaza de la República (Republic Plaza) include the National Palace of Culture (home to the National Museum), the Presidential Palace, a sports stadium, and Managua's Old Cathedral. The cathedral, though severely damaged and unusable, is being restored.

NO STREET SIGNS? NO PROBLEM

Because of the 1972 earthquake, Managua has few street signs and people rarely use them. Rather than providing the address of a person's house, residents of Managua instead give directions to the nearest landmark (such as a well-known building), followed by the number of blocks that should be traveled and in which direction. The directions are *al lago* (toward the lake to the north of the city), *al sur* (to the south), *arriba* (up, or east, where the sun comes up), and *abajo* (down, or west, where the sun goes down).

Although the city's downtown was never rebuilt, Managua has continued to grow. After the earthquake, new business and residential areas sprung up on the outskirts of downtown Managua. Over time these areas took on a life of their own. Managua has since become a collection of suburbs, each with its own social and economic structure.

LEÓN (population 168,000) was originally founded by Spanish explorers in 1524. It was initially located at the foot of Momotombo Volcano. When an earthquake destroyed León in 1610, Spanish colonists moved the city to its present site about 30 miles (48 km) northwest of Managua. León is considered the intellectual capital of the nation, as well as an industrial and commercial center. The city revolves around its university, founded in 1812. León's architecture has a colonial feel, and adobe homes with red-tiled roofs line narrow streets.

GRANADA (population 95,000) also dates its founding to 1524. But its location at the foot of another volcano, Mombacho, has remained unchanged. Granada has long been a wealthy trading center and remains the commercial heart of a region of farms and cattle ranches.

The second Catedral de Granada was finished in 1915. In 1856 a conquering army destroyed the first cathedral. It had been built in 1583.

It has also become a popular tourist destination. Like León, Granada has many colonial-era structures.

CHINANDEGA (population 147,000) lies to the north, midway between León and the Honduran border. Chinandega is in an agricultural region that produces grain, bananas, peanuts, and sugarcane.

MASAYA (population 129,000) lies on the slopes of the Masaya Volcano, nearly halfway between Managua and Granada. Many of Nicaragua's export items—including coffee, sugar, beef, bananas, and tobacco—are traded here before entering the world market. Masaya is also the center of Nicaragua's folk culture.

OTHER CITIES Estelí (population 111,000) and Matagalpa (population 86,000) are the largest cities in Nicaragua's central region. Matagalpa is the center of Nicaragua's coffee-growing region, while the tobacco that grows around Estelí goes into some of the world's finest cigars. Puerto Cabezas (population 42,600) and Bluefields (population 37,900), both located on the Caribbean coast, are the largest cities in the Caribbean Lowlands region.

Visit www.vgsbooks.com for links to more photographs from Nicaragua and more information about its cities, geography, and flora and fauna.

HISTORY AND GOVERNMENT

Historians and archaeologists (scholars who study early human cultures) have dated human habitation in Nicaragua as far back as 12,000 B.C. The earliest humans in the region were nomadic hunter-gatherers. They moved from one region to the next in search of food, such as fruits, roots, and animals. These early human inhabitants built homes of bark, made clothing from animal hides, and crafted tools from stone and clay.

By 1000 B.C., early Central Americans were living in permanent villages. Several distinct tribal nations had emerged. A chieftain, known as a cacique, headed each group. These native peoples traded with one another and with groups to the north and south. They traveled into present-day Mexico and along the Pacific and Atlantic coasts of South America using seagoing boats and footpaths that crisscrossed the region's mountains and forests.

A number of early cultures thrived in Nicaragua. Among the largest groups were the Nicarao and the Chorotega. Archaeologists believe these groups—often called Indians—moved southward into the Pacific Lowlands and Central Highlands during the A.D. 1200s. Both groups shared similarities with the native peoples of Mexico and Guatemala, including language, culture, and religion. The Nicarao and Chorotega spoke versions of a language known as Nahuatl. They survived by hunting and by growing crops, such as corn, beans, chili peppers, and avocados. These peoples also practiced traditional religions that involved spirit and ancestor worship.

Along the Caribbean coast, early native groups—among them the Bawihka, the Sumu, and the Rama—were more closely related to the early inhabitants of present-day Colombia. Tribes here spoke a language with ties to that of the Chibcha Indians of Colombia. Early natives hunted, fished, and grew crops, such as cassava and plantains. The people of this region also appear to have connections to the native peoples of the Caribbean Islands.

Spanish Conquest

Europeans were introduced to Central America by the Italian explorer Christopher Columbus. His fourth and final voyage to the Americas took place in 1502. While searching for a western sea route to India, Columbus spent two months exploring the coasts of Nicaragua, Costa Rica, and Honduras. His reports back to the king and queen of Spain, who sponsored his voyages, told of a land rich in gold. These reports led to further Spanish exploration of the region.

The Spanish conquest of present-day Nicaragua began in 1522 with an expedition by conquistador (conqueror) Gil González Dávila. González Dávila launched his expedition from present-day Panama. During the expedition, he and his men encountered members of the Nicarao. They introduced the Nicarao to their own Roman Catholic religion and returned to Panama with gold ornaments offered to them by tribal leaders. Other Indians were more resistant to the newcomers, however, and launched attacks against them.

A 1524 expedition from Panama, led by Francisco Hernández de Córdoba, established the first Spanish settlements in Nicaragua. During this expedition, Fernández de Córdoba founded the cities of Granada and León. Catholic priests came to settle with the Spanish conquistadors and spread their faith among the native peoples.

In Granada, a statue of **Fernández de Córdoba** faces inland from the shore of Lake Nicaragua.

Shortly after Spanish settlements had been established in Nicaragua, Hernán Cortés, the Spanish conqueror of Mexico, sent one of his lieutenants, Pedro de Alvarado, to claim the area. Alvarado opened up a transportation route from Granada to the Caribbean Sea. He also built forts at the mouth of the San Juan River and the adjoining lowland areas. But Spain's Nicaraguan colony struggled. Many settlers left Nicaragua to join efforts to conquer the Inca Empire in Peru. In 1543 Nicaragua became part of the Captaincy General of Guatemala, an administrative unit created by Spain to govern the region. The Captaincy General was divided into provinces that included southern Mexico and most of Central America, with its capital in Guatemala City. León became the capital of the province of Nicaragua.

Spanish rule brought Nicaragua the Roman Catholic faith, Spanish language and culture, and a European-style system of government. But with its limited land and small deposits of valuable minerals, Nicaragua did not attract many settlers. As a result, Spain largely ignored the small colony.

Read more about the colorful history of Nicaragua. Visit www.vgsbooks.com for links.

Colonial Life

Spanish settlers in Nicaragua lived mostly along the Pacific coast, on farms and ranches. They forced Indians or imported African slaves to work the land. These laborers farmed cacao beans (the source of cocoa) and indigo for export. They also raised other crops and herded cattle for the local population. To attract more new settlers to its struggling colonies in this region, Spain established a program called the *encomienda* system. An encomienda was a piece of land given to a settler. Along with the property, the settler also received the legal right to use local native peoples to work the land. The settlers promised payment and eventual freedom to the native peoples. In most cases, however, they held the native peoples as permanent, unpaid laborers—essentially slaves. Many native peoples died from harsh treatment, backbreaking labor, and diseases the settlers had brought from Europe. Others were sent to work in Spain's other colonies in the New World of the Americas.

Because Spain paid relatively little attention to its Central American colonies, Nicaragua remained poor and isolated throughout the seventeenth and eighteenth centuries. In addition, natural disasters, including powerful earthquakes in 1648, 1651, and 1663,

PIRATES OF THE CARIBBEAN

English, French, and Dutch pirates frequently raided the towns of colonial Nicaragua. In 1668 and again in 1670, English pirates attacked Granada. They looted its stores of gold and indigo, burned the city, and carried their spoils off to Europe. Pirates knew that the Spanish believed Nicaragua was not rich enough to need its own fortifications. Instead, powerful forts at Veracruz (on Mexico's Caribbean coast) and Portobelo (in Panama) were relied upon to stop piracy. But they often failed. Looting was so free and easy in poorly defended Nicaragua that Dutch pirate Abraham Blauvelt was able to found his own settlement. He established Bluefields in 1633. Only in 1672 did Spain bother to build bigger forts at the mouth of the San Juan River. By then treaties with Great Britain had reduced the need for defense. But while the treaties helped end the piracy problem, they also provided Great Britain with a foothold in the area.

caused massive destruction. And pirates frequently raided the Caribbean coast. Nevertheless, Nicaragua was home to about 180,000 people by the end of the 1700s. Most of these residents were mestizos (people of mixed heritage). León was the center of political, administrative, cultural, and religious life in the colony. Granada, meanwhile, was the center of the colony's agricultural wealth. Because of its location on Lake Nicaragua, it was also an important trading post. As León and Granada grew, the wealthy merchants and landowners of the two towns began to develop a rivalry.

The Spanish built few settlements along the Caribbean coast. That allowed the British (who had their own colonies in the Caribbean) to form an alliance with the Miskito Indians. Miskitos were the offspring of native peoples and African slaves who had escaped from England's Caribbean colonies. From then on, the Caribbean coast of Nicaragua became a battleground between Spanish and British interests.

◉ Independence

By the beginning of the nineteenth century, Nicaraguan mestizos had grown resentful of the Spanish-born population. They were unhappy that only Spanish-born individuals were allowed to govern the colony. Like other groups throughout the Americas, some Nicaraguans were deeply impressed by the success of the American Revolution (1775–1783). They began to consider becoming independent themselves. Spain was also experiencing its own turmoil, as wars in Europe weakened its hold over its Central American

One of the first battles *(above)* in the American Revolution was fought in Lexington, Massachusetts, on April 19, 1775. The American colonists' successful revolt against British rule inspired later independence movements in Central America.

colonies. These events combined to inspire a drive for independence throughout Spain's New World colonies. On September 15, 1821, all of the provinces within the Captaincy General of Guatemala—Nicaragua, Costa Rica, Guatemala, El Salvador, and Honduras—declared their independence from Spain.

During the next two decades, the newly independent provinces made several attempts to form a Central American union. In 1822 Central American leaders accepted an invitation from Mexican leader Agustín de Iturbide to join the Mexican Empire. But when Iturbide tried to use his troops to enforce Mexican dominance, the provinces resisted. In 1823 a congress in Guatemala City declared an end to the association with Mexico. Central American leaders established the United Provinces of Central America, a republic modeled after the United States of America.

But within Nicaragua and the other provinces, disagreements over the nature of the union led to conflict. In each country, views were split between two sets of political beliefs. Conservatives wanted the republic to have a strong central government. Liberals believed the individual provinces should have more power than the central government. Eventually, this conflict led to a civil war in the provinces. The war lasted for three years, from 1826 to 1829, but the disagreements continued beyond the end of the fighting. In 1838 Nicaragua—along with Costa Rica and Honduras—withdrew from the federation. Meanwhile, politicians in León and Granada fought for control of Nicaragua. León was the seat of the Liberals, while Conservatives controlled Granada.

Nicaragua experienced more problems in 1848 when British settlers seized the port of San Juan del Norte on the Caribbean coast and expelled all Nicaraguan officials. The following year, Britain forced

Nicaragua to sign a treaty recognizing British authority over the Miskito people.

CANAL DREAMS

From the time of the Spanish conquest, the rulers of Central America dreamed of a canal connecting the Atlantic and Pacific oceans. With a canal, ships would no longer have to make the long, dangerous journey around Cape Horn at the tip of South America. Central American leaders believed that a canal would make the region important to world trade. Foreign leaders and business owners also saw the potential for great wealth in building and controlling such a canal. Nicaragua was a natural choice for a canal location. Ships could take the San Juan River to Lake Managua, which a canal could connect to the Pacific. French, British, and U.S. agents all visited Nicaragua to investigate the possibilities. But these efforts all fell flat for a variety of reasons. Eventually, the United States did build a canal in Central America—but not in Nicaragua. Nicaragua's government insisted on control over any canal the United States might build there. So U.S. officials chose instead to build its canal in Panama.

◉ William Walker

Nicaragua's first few decades as an independent nation were stormy ones. By the end of the 1840s, so many male Nicaraguans had been killed in various Central American wars that women outnumbered men in some places by as many as five to one. Although the country's wealthy merchants and landowners were profiting from the export of cattle, indigo, and cacao, the majority of Nicaragua's 250,000 residents lived in poverty. With the discovery of gold in California in 1848, however, Nicaragua received an economic boost. Thousands of hopeful prospectors from the United States made their way to the California gold mines through Nicaragua. This southern route was safer and quicker than crossing the continental United States. U.S. tycoon Cornelius Vanderbilt constructed roads, railroads, and docks on both coasts to transport the gold seekers.

Meanwhile, Liberals and Conservatives continued to fight for control of the country. In 1854 General Fruto Chamorro, a Conservative, took over the Nicaraguan government and exiled leading Liberal opponents. The Liberals, looking to the United States for support, sought the help of William Walker, a U.S. adventurer and soldier. They offered him free land in Nicaragua if he would recruit a force to aid them in their battle against the Conservatives.

On arriving in Granada in 1855, **Walker's filibusters** lived in the San Francisco Convent, built in 1524.

Walker agreed, and in 1855 his band of fifty-eight adventurers—known as filibusters—captured the town of Rivas. Soon afterward they conquered Granada and threw out the Conservative government. Walker then set up a government headed by Liberal politician Patricio Rivas. But Walker, who wanted to rule the country himself, wasn't finished. In 1856 he held a rigged election in which he manipulated the results—and declared himself president. Among his first moves was to make English the official language of the country. He also legalized slavery.

Soon Nicaraguans—including the Liberals who had initially sought Walker's help—turned against him. They were joined by leaders from the other Central American countries, who feared that Walker would expand his control. The struggle against Walker became known as the National War (1856–1857). This bloody conflict resulted in the burning of Granada and the loss of thousands of Central American lives.

Walker's reign finally ended in 1857, when his forces were defeated at the town of Rivas. Walker surrendered to a U.S. naval officer there and was sent back to the United States. After his defeat, Walker made several attempts to return to Central America. But three years later, a Honduran firing squad captured and killed him.

The Late Nineteenth Century

A period of reconstruction followed the National War. In 1858 Nicaragua adopted a new constitution and made Managua the nation's capital. The location was a compromise between the Liberals of León and the Conservatives of Granada. The first president elected under the new constitution, Conservative Tomás Martínez, governed from 1859 to 1867. Martínez was followed by eight more presidents, all but one of whom served four-year terms.

Nicaragua saw economic development and modernization during this period. Coffee production, begun in the 1850s, expanded. Bananas also became an important export crop. European immigrants to Nicaragua brought new farming methods that boosted production. Railroad service began along the Pacific coast. Telegraph service began in 1876, and an underwater telegraph cable linked Nicaragua to the outside world in 1882. There was diplomatic success too. Under the 1880 Treaty of Managua, Great Britain surrendered all of its claims to the Mosquito Coast (Carribean Lowlands). Residents there continued to be independent of the Nicaraguan government for another fourteen years, however.

This era of peace came to an end in 1895. That year the Liberal general José Santos Zelaya took power by force. Zelaya's rule brought more material progress. He opened the country to foreign investment, extended the country's railways, built new roads and port facilities, and increased coffee production and banana exports. He established public schools, as well. But Zelaya was also corrupt and ruthless. He used his power to enrich himself and his supporters, and to persecute and harass his Conservative foes. Many of Zelaya's opponents fled the country.

Meanwhile, many U.S. companies were becoming involved in the Nicaraguan economy. They were eager to take advantage of the nation's cheap land and low labor costs. By the early 1900s, U.S. companies controlled most of Nicaragua's production of coffee, bananas, gold, and timber.

Zelaya was firmly opposed to growing U.S. involvement in Central America. This stance made him especially unpopular with U.S. leaders. In order to help Zelaya's opponents remove him from office, the United States landed four hundred Marines at Bluefields on the Caribbean coast in 1909. Zelaya fled into exile, leaving his country in a state of disorder.

The United States Intervenes

Zelaya's departure created political chaos over the next few years. At first, Conservative Juan Estrada was elected president with the backing of the United States. But Liberals revolted when Estrada's vice president, Adolfo Díaz, became president in 1912. U.S. Marines returned again to restore order, ending the revolt and keeping Díaz in office.

U.S. Marines take aim against Nicaraguan rebels in 1912.

U.S. involvement in Nicaragua extended beyond its military presence. Its economic hold over the country was still growing. Like many Central American nations, Nicaragua borrowed from the United States and European nations to modernize its infrastructure (basic systems such as transportation). It remained deep in debt to those countries. Under the 1911 Knox-Castillo Treaty, the U.S. government promised to loan Nicaragua $15 million. In return, the U.S. government received the right to protect U.S. business interests in Nicaragua. Loans from New York banks helped Nicaragua pay off its debts but also strengthened U.S. control of the country. Then, in 1916, the Chamorro-Bryan Treaty gave the United States a claim to any future canal route by way of the San Juan River. The treaty also ensured that no foreign power could build a waterway in Nicaragua to compete with the U.S.-owned Panama Canal. In return, the U.S. government paid Nicaragua $3 million.

In 1925 U.S. president Calvin Coolidge decided that it was safe to pull the Marines out of Nicaragua. But they would not be gone for long. The Liberals and Conservatives renewed their civil war when Liberal politician Juan Bautista Sacasa led a rebellion against the Díaz government. President Coolidge, who feared that a Liberal government would not be good for U.S. interests in Nicaragua, sent battleships into Nicaraguan waters. They landed two thousand Marines and delivered arms to Díaz's troops. The United States also began training a Nicaraguan national guard. The intended role of the Guardia Nacional was to maintain peace in the country—but also to protect U.S. interests.

The Sandino Revolt

In 1927 U.S. diplomats convinced Liberals and Conservatives to agree to a peace deal known as the Espino Negro Pact. The pact allowed

President Díaz to remain in office until elections could be held in 1928. But the deal was resisted by General Augusto César Sandino, a Liberal who fiercely opposed the U.S. military occupation. Sandino launched a revolt against the Nicaraguan government and U.S. forces with a handful of poorly equipped troops. Sandino's fight against the Americans made him a hero to many Nicaraguans.

Sandino and his men fought the Marines until 1933, when U.S. president Franklin D. Roosevelt decided to pull all U.S. forces out of Nicaragua. The same year, Juan B. Sacasa became Nicaragua's new president. After the departure of U.S. forces, Sandino laid down his arms voluntarily and agreed to meet with President Sacasa. Among Sandino's demands was the disbanding of the Guardia Nacional. He opposed the guard because of its connection to the U.S. military. By then the Guardia Nacional and its leader, General Anastasio "Tacho" Somoza García, had become a very powerful force in the country. In 1934 officers of the Guardia Nacional, acting under the orders of Somoza, arrested and executed Sandino.

The Somoza Dynasty

Following Sandino's execution, General Somoza launched a campaign to wipe out all of Sandino's supporters and to win support from the country's Liberals. Soon he had become the most powerful man in Nicaragua. Eventually, Somoza used the power of the Guardia Nacional to remove Sacasa from office and clear the way for his own election as president in 1937.

Then, in 1938, Somoza declared his intention to stay in power beyond one term. Somoza promptly established a dictatorship—a government in which he alone wielded power. As president and head of the military, Somoza had complete control over the country. He used his power to enrich both his family and his political allies. His vast wealth enabled him to pay off political opponents.

Somoza also used his power to modernize Nicaragua, improve the economy, and encourage foreign investment. Nevertheless, over time, opposition to his dictatorship grew both inside and outside of Nicaragua. Criticism increased when Somoza announced he would run for reelection in 1944. In response, Somoza created a series of puppet governments—administrations in which he maintained power from behind the scenes. Despite these efforts, everyone knew who was in power. Many foreign nations refused to recognize his government. And because Somoza controlled the military, neither the Liberals nor the Conservatives could remove him from office. After his reelection in a rigged election in 1950, Somoza made a series of constitutional reforms that eliminated presidential elections altogether.

Tacho Somoza (left) rides beside U.S. president Franklin D. Roosevelt (right) during a 1939 visit to the United States. Roosevelt was president from 1933 to 1945.

Somoza made many political ene-mies during his years in power. In 1956 a young Nicaraguan poet, Rigoberto López Pérez, assassinated him. But Somoza's son, Luis Somoza Debayle, stepped in to finish his father's presidential term. The next year, Luis Somoza was elected president.

Luis Somoza made some minor democratic reforms. Critics of the government were allowed greater freedom of speech. And to the sur-prise of many Nicaraguans, the new president requested that the Nicaraguan congress formally block his own reelection for a second term.

THE STRONGMAN SOMOZA

Tacho Somoza was once quoted as saying, "Nicaragua es mi finca" (Nicaragua is my farm). The statement was almost literally true. He owned 10 to 15 percent of all farmland in Nicaragua. At his death, his personal fortune was worth between $60 and $300 million. Although Tacho Somoza used his power to enrich himself, he also used it to modernize his country. He built schools, hospitals, and hydroelectric plants. He worked to improve Nicaraguan agriculture, expand the nation's produc-tion of beef, and draw on the nation's gold resources. In addition, Somoza's pro-American policies helped attract U.S. investment and boost Nicaragua's economy. Outsiders often praised his success in improving the nation's network of roads. Critics, however, claimed that all Nicaraguan roads seemed to lead to a Somoza family farm.

Tacho Somoza was not generally considered a cruel man. He saw himself as a generous leader preparing his people for democracy. His opponents, however, saw him as a greedy, corrupt tyrant.

True to his word, Somoza stepped down at the end of his first term. But he used his family's influence to back his own candidate in the 1963 election. The candidate, René Schick Gutíerrez, was a long-time employee of the Somoza regime. Despite this influence, the elections were reported to be as honest as Nicaragua had ever held. Schick won an overwhelming victory, but he died of natural causes in 1966.

In 1967 Tachito Somoza, the youngest son of Tacho Somoza and the brother of Luis Somoza Debayle, ran for president. The outcome of the election was never in doubt. In addition to his family connections, Tachito Somoza was the chief director of the Guardia Nacional. During the campaign, the guard harassed and imprisoned supporters of the opposing candidate, Fernando Agüero. Tachito Somoza, who pledged to continue the more democratic policies of his brother, entered office at the age of forty-one. Like his father, he held the position of president and head of the military.

With Tachito Somoza as president, the Somoza family's control over the Nicaraguan economy expanded. By the early 1970s, the Somozas operated a wide variety of businesses. These included ranches to raise cattle and meat-packing plants to prepare them for market, extensive coffee and cotton plantations, banks, hotels, newspapers, television stations, and Nicaragua's only cement factory. They also operated the nation's only shipping line and the national airline.

The 1972 Earthquake

Although Tachito Somoza obeyed the ban against successive presidential terms, he did not pass his power to an elected successor. Instead, he handed power to a three-man junta (a ruling council) in 1972. This body of two Liberal politicians and one Conservative was to govern the country until presidential elections could be held in 1974. By then opposition to Somoza's corrupt and oppressive rule was growing. While the Somoza family and its friends grew wealthier, the majority of Nicaraguans remained poor. Most citizens had little access to proper housing, health care, and education. Members of the press and the Catholic Church began to speak out against the Somoza-run government.

Then, on December 23, 1972, a violent earthquake struck the city of Managua. The earthquake killed ten thousand people, injured many more, and destroyed fifty thousand homes. Downtown Managua was particularly hard hit. More than 80 percent of the city's commercial buildings were destroyed. The day after the earthquake, Tachito Somoza appointed himself president of the national emergency committee. He also declared martial law—a move that put the

The **1972 earthquake in Managua** measured 6.3 on the Richter scale of earthquake intensity. On the Richter scale, 5 is ten thousand times stronger than 4, and 6 is ten thousand times greater than 5. Shaking that people notice occurs in an earthquake that measures about 4.5 on the scale.

military in charge of the country. As head of the military, Tachito Somoza became the country's unofficial leader.

The 1972 earthquake revealed the corruption of the Somoza government to the world. According to numerous reports, members of the Guardia Nacional sold foreign aid supplies that had been donated to the country. They also demanded bribes to guard damaged properties, to obtain reconstruction permits and import licenses, and to win government contracts for rebuilding. Members of Tachito Somoza's administration even kept some foreign aid money for themselves. As owners of the only cement plant in Nicaragua, the Somoza family also made huge profits from rebuilding efforts.

The Sandinista Revolution

In the years following the earthquake, Nicaraguans grew increasingly unhappy with the Somoza government. Press reports of Tachito Somoza's corruption fueled the public's anger. In response, he announced a state of siege in 1975. This move allowed the government to censor the press and to suspend the civil rights of Nicaraguan citizens. Members of the Guardia Nacional persecuted those suspected of anti-Somoza activities. Human rights violations against civilians brought strong criticism from the Catholic Church and from international human rights groups such as Amnesty International. Even the United States, which had long ignored the corruption of the Somoza regime, stated its concern.

In reaction to Tachito Somoza's policies, a revolutionary movement took shape. Important business leaders and academics began forming anti-Somoza alliances. The strongest opposition group was the Sandinista National Liberation Front (FSLN), more commonly known as the Sandinistas. Nicaraguan revolutionary Carlos Fonseca had founded the FSLN—named after Augusto César Sandino, the resistance leader of the 1920s and 1930s—in the early 1960s. By 1975 the Sandinistas had gained enough support from rural Nicaraguans and student groups to launch a military campaign against the government. Tensions in the country ran high, and Nicaraguans began to fear a civil war.

The spark that finally touched off the revolution occurred on January 9, 1978. On that day, Pedro Joaquín Chamorro, the editor of Managua's *La Prensa* newspaper, was killed. The paper had been highly critical of Tachito Somoza, and evidence soon surfaced that the Somoza government had played a role in Chamorro's killing. The day after the

Sandinista rebels took to the streets in a building-to-building fight against government troops in 1978.

assassination, thirty thousand people demonstrated in the streets of Managua. Some attacked and burned buildings that housed Somoza-connected businesses. From then on, Nicaraguan workers and students held increasingly larger strikes and clashed frequently with the Guardia Nacional. Thousands of young men and women joined the Sandinista army. Fighting between the Sandinistas and the government increased.

The final military offensive by the Sandinistas began in 1979. It consisted of coordinated attacks throughout the country. Fighting erupted in the streets of Managua and other cities, including Matagalpa, Estelí, León, and Masaya. Eventually Sandinista fighters began to overwhelm government forces. Tachito Somoza looked for support from the United States, but by then the U.S. government had stopped providing military assistance to the Nicaraguan government. In fact, on June 27, 1979, a new U.S. ambassador arrived in Managua with instructions to secure Somoza's resignation. With ammunition running out, Tachito Somoza fled the country on July 17. He would be assassinated in Paraguay the next year.

The Sandinistas in Power

The Sandinistas took over a crippled country and a divided people. From 30,000 to 50,000 Nicaraguans had been killed during the Sandinista-Somoza conflict. Another 100,000 had been wounded, and more than 600,000 were homeless. The economy was devastated.

A ruling body known as the Junta of National Reconstruction led the new Sandinista government. It immediately began making economic and social reforms. One of the government's first moves was to confiscate 2 million acres (809,400 hectares) of land that had been owned by the Somoza family. The aim was to distribute this land to the rural poor. The new government then began to nationalize the economy by taking over banks, mines, and factories. In addition, the Sandinistas launched a massive literacy campaign. Thousands of volunteers went to rural areas to teach reading, writing, and basic math skills. The government also promised to end the human rights violations that had taken place under the Somoza government.

The leaders of the Sandinista government were partly inspired by Communism. This political system is based on the idea of shared property and state control of the economy. As a result, the Sandinistas received assistance from many Communist countries during their first years in power. Cuba supplied Nicaragua with two thousand teachers and military advisers. And the Soviet Union agreed to send technical experts to develop the battered Nicaraguan economy. While this support helped Nicaragua, it worried U.S. politicians who feared the spread of Communism in Central America.

These fears increased when Cuba's Communist leader, Fidel Castro, took part in ceremonies marking the first anniversary of the Sandinista revolution. By the second anniversary, the U.S. Congress had stopped providing economic aid to Nicaragua because the Sandinistas were allegedly supplying arms to a rebel movement in El Salvador. By the third anniversary in 1982, the U.S. government was portraying Nicaragua's growing military as a threat to peace in Central America. The United States and other nations also accused the Sandinistas of burning down the homes of Miskito Indians in eastern Nicaragua and driving them into refugee camps in neighboring Honduras.

The Contra Rebellion

By 1982 the Sandinista government found itself under heavy criticism. Many Nicaraguans were unhappy with the revolution and its direction. Critics included poor farmers whose lives had not improved, members of the business community, the press, and former supporters of the Somoza family. In addition, former members of the Guardia Nacional began to organize their own rebel guerrilla forces with military and financial support from the United States. Operating from bases in neighboring Costa Rica and Honduras, these *Contrarevolucionarios* (Contras) began launching military raids into Nicaraguan territory.

The Contras were highly unpopular with many Nicaraguans because of their connection to the Somoza government. But they still posed a serious threat to the Sandinista government. Sandinista leadership responded by clamping down on all political opposition. Critics began to suggest that the Sandinistas were no better than Somoza.

Daniel Ortega Saavedra

In response, the Sandinistas agreed to hold national elections on November 4, 1984. Sandinista leader Daniel Ortega Saavedra won the election with 63 percent of the popular vote. Observers said the elections were fair, but the major opposition parties refused to participate in them. They claimed the Sandinista government had created a climate of fear. Despite the protests, Daniel Ortega was sworn in as Nicaragua's new president on January 10, 1985. The elections also gave the Sandinistas a two-thirds majority in the National Assembly, where laws are approved.

But the country's civil war continued. The threat from the Contras forced the Sandinista government to spend more than one-quarter of the national budget on defense. Then, in 1985, the United States stopped all trade with Nicaragua. The move crippled the Nicaraguan economy. By 1986 the nation was largely dependent on aid from the Soviet Union and it had lost more than ten thousand people in the war.

Peace and a New Democratic Era

In February 1987, Costa Rican president Oscar Arias Sánchez put forth a peace proposal to end the fighting in Nicaragua. The Arias Plan called for a cease-fire between the Sandinista government and the Contras. The plan also called for free elections and other democratic reforms. On August 7, 1987, leaders from Honduras, El Salvador, Nicaragua, Guatemala, and Costa Rica met to sign the agreement.

To meet the terms of the peace deal, the Sandinista government signed a cease-fire with the Contras in 1988. The Sandinistas also announced presidential elections for early 1990. In response, fourteen Conservative and Liberal opposition parties came together to form the National Opposition Union (UNO). This group supported Violeta Barrios de Chamorro. Violeta Chamorro was the editor of *La Prensa* and the widow of slain journalist Pedro Chamorro. Although she had no formal political training, she overcame the well-organized Sandinista campaign and defeated Daniel Ortega for the presidency. International observers said it was a free and fair election. Despite their loss at the polls, many Sandinista officials remained in powerful government positions.

NICARAGUA AND THE UNITED STATES

The United States was frequently involved in Nicaraguan affairs during the twentieth century, for a variety of reasons. Many people feel that U.S. involvement in the early 1900s was an example of "dollar diplomacy," in which U.S. troops were called on not only to settle the country's political disputes but also to protect U.S. investments in Nicaragua's gold mines, plantations, railways, and banks. In the 1980s, Nicaragua was a battlefield in the Cold War (1945–1991)—a nonmilitary conflict between the United States and the Soviet Union. U.S. leaders did not want to see Communism spreading anywhere in the world, particularly in Central America. They feared that Communist governments in Nicaragua and other Central American countries would give the Soviet Union influence over the region. Although Nicaragua is presently on friendly terms with the United States, some Nicaraguans still resent the U.S. role in their country's history.

During the 1990 election, newspaper editor Violeta Chamorro campaigned for the Nicaraguan presidency on street corners.

After the election, President Chamorro faced the task of rebuilding a shattered nation. She started by reducing the size of the Sandinista army and disarming the Contras. She encouraged the international community to help rebuild the country. She began to privatize the economy by selling state-held companies to private investors. Not all of her efforts were successful, however. For example, her attempt to redistribute land seized by the Sandinistas during the 1980s ran into problems. Peasants and landowners disputed their claims. Much of the land was held by former Sandinista officials who refused to turn it over. In addition, Chamorro's acceptance of Sandinistas in the new government angered many of her supporters. Chamorro broke with the UNO in January 1993. She chose not to run for a second term.

In 1996 Arnoldo Alemán—the presidential candidate for the Liberal Alliance—defeated former president Daniel Ortega in a peaceful election. Alemán faced many problems. Challenges included a weak economy, high foreign and domestic debt, and renewed clashes between former Contras and the Sandinista-led Nicaraguan army. But in 1997, the Alemán government reached an agreement with many of the armed groups that still roamed the country. These groups broke up soon afterward. Alemán also made a number of economic reforms, creating programs to encourage more trade with other nations—particularly the United States. The country's economy slowly began to improve.

Hurricane Mitch

Nicaragua's journey to stability took a major blow when Hurricane Mitch hit in October 1998. Over a period of ten days, the hurricane battered Nicaragua and its neighbors. Mitch dumped huge amounts of rain in the northern and northwestern areas of the country. The rain caused massive flooding. Huge mudslides wiped out entire villages. By the time the storm had finally passed, nearly 4,000 people had been killed. Nearly 800,000 were homeless. And shortages of food and water led to many more deaths in the weeks and months following Hurricane Mitch. In addition, the storm destroyed crops and farmland, causing massive damage to the nation's fragile economy. More than 30 percent of Nicaragua's coffee crop was wiped out. Bean, sugarcane, and banana crops were severely damaged. More than 70 percent of the country's infrastructure was devastated. Overall, the storm caused an estimated $1.5 billion in damage.

The devastation caused by Mitch was a huge setback for the Nicaraguan economy. In the early 2000s, Nicaragua continued to struggle with high levels of unemployment and debt. Its people also faced an extreme inequality in the distribution of income. While a few Nicaraguans are wealthy, many still suffer from unemployment or underemployment and live in poverty. Because economic growth continues to be too low to meet the country's needs, Nicaragua still relies heavily on foreign aid. This pattern only pushes the nation further into debt. In 2004 Nicaragua qualified for nearly $4 billion in foreign debt reduction from the International Monetary Fund (IMF) under a program known as the Heavily Indebted Poor Countries Initiative. This program aims to reduce the foreign debt of the world's poorest nations. Meanwhile, some positive economic signs include a decrease in inflation and a more stable currency.

One factor that the Nicaraguan government hopes will help the economy is the approval of the Dominican Republic-Central America Free Trade Agreement (DR-CAFTA). Nicaragua signed this trade deal in 2004 after

THE INTERNATIONAL MONETARY FUND

The International Monetary Fund is closely connected to the World Bank, an agency of the United Nations that gives loans to UN member nations. The IMF offers policy advice to countries willing to change their economic policies. For instance, the IMF may insist that a country in financial difficulty take steps to reduce its debts and inflation. These policies may cause economic hardships at first but are designed to create long-term economic stability.

several years of negotiation, and the National Assembly later approved it. The goal of DR-CAFTA is to create a free trade zone that would include Costa Rica, Honduras, Guatemala, El Salvador, the Dominican Republic, and the United States. If passed by the congresses of all the nations involved, the agreement will allow member nations to export products to one another without having to pay taxes on them.

Supporters of the free trade agreement known as **DR-CAFTA** believe it will create jobs and improve living conditions in Nicaragua by encouraging foreign investment. Opponents worry that the agreement will allow foreign companies to take advantage of Nicaragua's less strict labor and environmental laws, and that Nicaraguan workers will be poorly paid and poorly treated. They also worry that the nation's farmers will be wiped out by competition with cheap imports from large U.S. agriculture companies.

Although Nicaragua's political situation is far less chaotic than it has been, the nation continues to experience growing pains as a democracy. Corruption and political rivalry within the government remain. For example, in 2002 Arnoldo Alemán was succeeded by his vice president, Enrique Bolaños Geyer. But in 2003, Bolaños broke with his party, the Liberal Constitutional Party (PLC). Bolaños then launched an anticorruption campaign that led to the arrest and imprisonment of the former president for fraud. The move cost Bolaños the support of politicians loyal to Alemán. Since then his presidency has been marked by political standoffs with the National Assembly.

In late 2004, Bolaños's opposition revised the country's constitution to give the National Assembly final approval over the appointment of cabinet members and ambassadors. Bolaños and his government rejected those reforms, arguing that they would weaken the president's authority. The standoff between the government and the National Assembly continued into 2005, with the opposition calling for Bolaños to resign.

◉ Government

The Nicaraguan government is divided into four branches. The executive branch consists of the president, the vice president, and an appointed cabinet (group of advisers). The president is elected by popular vote for a five-year term and serves as both the chief of state and the head of government. The legislative branch of the government is the National Assembly. This body is also elected by popular vote. All adult men and women in Nicaragua are eligible to vote.

The judicial branch of government includes a Supreme Court and appeals, district, and local courts. Supreme Court justices are elected for five-year terms by the National Assembly. Separate judges handle labor and administrative matters.

The fourth branch of government is the Supreme Electoral Council. This branch is responsible for organizing and holding elections.

Nicaragua is divided into fifteen geographic departments: Boaco, Carazo, Chinandega, Chontales, Estelí, Granada, Jinotega, León, Madriz, Managua, Masaya, Matagalpa, Nueva Segovia, Río San Juan, and Rivas. The country's two autonomous (self-governing) regions are the Northern Atlantic Autonomous Region and the Southern Atlantic Autonomous Region.

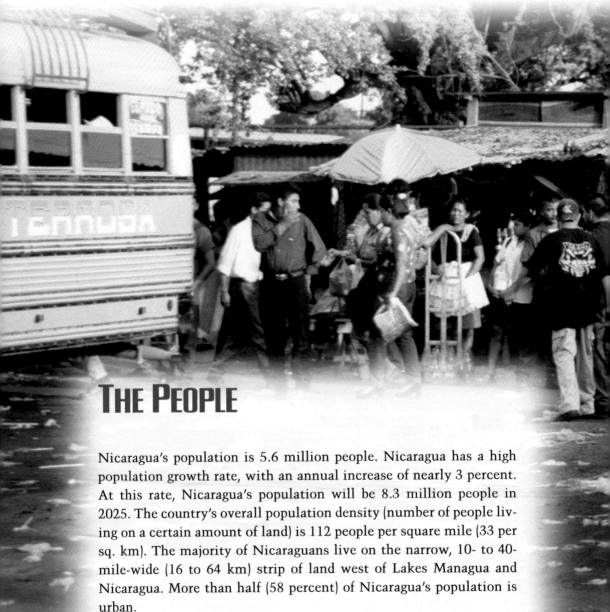

THE PEOPLE

Nicaragua's population is 5.6 million people. Nicaragua has a high population growth rate, with an annual increase of nearly 3 percent. At this rate, Nicaragua's population will be 8.3 million people in 2025. The country's overall population density (number of people living on a certain amount of land) is 112 people per square mile (33 per sq. km). The majority of Nicaraguans live on the narrow, 10- to 40-mile-wide (16 to 64 km) strip of land west of Lakes Managua and Nicaragua. More than half (58 percent) of Nicaragua's population is urban.

Many adult Nicaraguans were killed in the conflicts of the 1970s and 1980s. As a result, Nicaragua has the youngest population of any Central American nation, with 43 percent of its people less than 15 years of age. The average life expectancy for Nicaraguans is 69 years.

The devastation caused by years of conflict has taken its toll on Nicaraguan society. The country faces many social problems, including high unemployment and widespread poverty. Although the

web enhanced @ www.vgsbooks.com

government has made strides in fighting poverty and has improved the nation's educational and health-care systems, it still has much work to do.

Racial Makeup

People of European ancestry dominate Nicaragua's population. Approximately 69 percent of Nicaragua's population is mestizo, a result of the racial mixing between Europeans and native peoples. This blending began shortly after the arrival of the first Spanish colonists and has continued ever since. Another 17 percent of Nicaragua's population is classified as white. These people are of pure Spanish blood or are descendants of immigrants from other European lands. Many Germans came to Nicaragua in the mid-1800s seeking opportunity in Nicaragua's coffee and banana industries.

Black Nicaraguans make up 9 percent of the population. Black Nicaraguans live mainly along the Caribbean coast. Most are the

Black students in Bluefields on Nicaragua's east coast pause for a photograph.

descendants of Afro-Caribbean slaves who came to Nicaragua from the islands of Jamaica and Haiti during the colonial era. Some are more recent immigrants from other islands of the West Indies. Nicaragua's black population also includes Creoles—the descendants of blacks who mixed with Spanish and English colonists. Another group, the Garífuna, are descended from a mix of Caribbean native peoples and African slaves.

Native groups make up 5 percent of the Nicaraguan population and also live mainly along the Caribbean coast. These groups include the Miskito Indians, a group that shares traces of African and English blood. Miskito Indians live along Nicaragua's Caribbean coast, from the city of Bluefields to the Coco River along the Honduran frontier. The Sumu people generally live north of Bluefields. The Rama Indians, the smallest of Nicaragua's native groups, live south of Bluefields. They have maintained many of their traditional ways, using traditional tools to fish and grow crops.

◉ Education

Nicaragua's educational system has made great strides since the end of the Somoza dynasty. Some credit for this improvement goes to the Sandinista government's national literacy campaign in the early 1980s. Nicaraguan government figures indicate that 68 percent of all Nicaraguans aged 15 and older are literate, compared to only 50 percent at the end of the Somoza dynasty. The numbers are even higher among young people, with 87 percent of Nicaraguans between the ages of 15 and 24 being literate. The Sandinista government provided free primary and secondary education. Since the late 1990s, however, the government has charged families a fee.

The school year in Nicaragua runs from February to October, with a three-month break beginning in November. Primary school attendance is officially required for children from 7 to 12 years of age. About 80 percent of primary-aged students do attend classes, but only about 70 percent complete primary school. Secondary schools instruct students for another five years, starting at the age of 13. Only 54 percent of Nicaraguan youth attend secondary school. In general, school attendance rates are lower for children in rural areas. As in other Central American nations, many students end their studies before reaching the age of 18. They leave school so that they can work and support their families.

For students who want to continue their education beyond secondary school, Nicaragua has several postsecondary options. The National Autonomous University of Nicaragua is the country's oldest institution of higher learning and its largest public university. It has seven thousand students at campuses in León and Managua. Central American University in Managua is run by Roman Catholic priests. Managua is also home to the National University of Engineering, where students study architecture and engineering, and the National University of Agriculture. Numerous technical and vocational schools offer professional training to students.

◎ Health

Health care has also improved in Nicaragua since the Somoza era. The Sandinista government created a ministry of health to manage the nation's health-care system and built new public clinics. The number of doctors, nurses, and hospitals increased. Preventive and primary medical care were emphasized. Overall, the Sandinista government left behind a greatly improved health-care system.

A **pharmacy** at a busy intersection is open for business in León. To read more about health and education in Nicaragua and to view the nation's latest population statistics go to www.vgsbooks.com for links.

LAND MINE LEGACY

One of the most frightening reminders of the fighting between the Sandinistas and the Contras is the number of land mines (explosive devices planted in the ground) left over from the conflict. Nicaragua has more land mines than any other country in the Western Hemisphere. More than forty-five thousand lie buried around the northern countryside. Their presence in certain rural areas prevents the further development of those communities. International teams of explosives experts have been working to remove the mines since the early 1990s. In addition, the Organization of American States (OAS) has organized a land mine awareness campaign aimed at the rural population. The campaign uses comic books with a story line discussing the dangers of land mines.

But quality health care is still lacking in much of Nicaragua, especially outside of the cities. While wealthy Nicaraguans can pay for private medical treatment, nearly 90 percent of the population relies on public health care. Public facilities are usually understaffed and poorly equipped. The government spends about 8 percent of its income on health services, or about $13 per individual—the lowest rate in Central America.

Because of the lack of quality health care outside of Managua, many people in Nicaragua continue to suffer from intestinal diseases such as malaria and cholera. These illnesses are caused by the country's tropical climate and unhealthy sanitary conditions. Another cause is the lack of reliable sources of clean water. One-fifth of Nicaraguans do not have access to safe drinking water. Malnutrition is also a problem, especially among children in rural areas. But Nicaragua has seen a decrease in childhood diseases such as typhoid, polio, and measles. These illnesses have been nearly eliminated through improved vaccination. In addition, the number of Nicaraguans living with HIV (human immunodeficiency virus, the virus that causes acquired immuno deficiency syndrome, or AIDS) is just over six thousand—a low number in Central America. Infant mortality (the number of babies who die within a year of their birth) stands at 30 for every 1,000 babies born. That number has dropped dramatically since the 1980s.

However, health and reproductive statistics vary greatly between rural and urban areas. For example, infant mortality rates are much higher among the rural poor than among urban residents. Many more rural children also suffer from diarrhea and upper respiratory infections. On average, Nicaraguan women will have 3.4 children in their lifetime, but women in rural areas tend to have 6 or more children because they have less access to birth control. Another problem in Nicaragua is the maternal mortality rate—the number of women who die during childbirth. An average of 230 women die during childbirth for every 100,000 babies born. In the isolated Caribbean Lowlands region, the maternal mortality rate is nearly twice that number.

Standard of Living

In general, the highest level of poverty in Nicaragua is in the country's rural areas, where many people live on less than one dollar a day. There are sharp differences between the lives of urban and rural Nicaraguans. Many of the conveniences of the city are unavailable to rural residents. Public transportation is difficult and sometimes nonexistent. Roofs of thin metal or of palm leaves protect homes in rural areas, and some villages have no electricity. Clean water for drinking and cooking, as well as proper sanitation facilities, is hard to find, and health clinics are few and far between. Some of the worst living conditions of all are found along the Caribbean coast, where many black Nicaraguans are culturally isolated from the rest of society.

The term *campesino*, which means "simple farmer" in Spanish, is often used to refer to rural Nicaraguans. Some campesinos survive through subsistence farming—growing only enough food to feed themselves. Others work on the large farms that produce much of the country's harvests. The greatest poverty in Nicaragua and some of the highest rates of illness can be found in the campesino population.

But Nicaragua's cities, which are expanding as the rural poor migrate for work, also have their problems. Issues facing Managua include poor infrastructure, high crime, and large slums. These run-down housing areas are home to unemployed or underemployed people living in ramshackle housing. Children from the slums are often forced to work at an early age, selling items in the city's marketplaces. Some of these children are on their own and survive through petty thievery, prostitution, and scrounging for food from the city's garbage dumps. Drug use among Nicaragua's street kids is becoming a growing problem.

CULTURAL LIFE

Despite the hardships their country has faced, the people of Nicaragua have created a culture reflecting the landscape's vibrancy and variety. But their cultural life also expresses their country's joys and sorrows. The capital city of Managua is a bustling place. Nicaraguan art, poetry, music, and other media reflect the country's energetic and sometimes chaotic lifestyle.

In contrast, cities such as León and Granada have a more relaxed atmosphere. The cultural life in these regions is similar to that of other Latin American countries. People enjoy long meals, especially a hearty lunch of rice and beans and a meat dish. After lunch it is common to take a siesta (rest) before heading back to work. Although life in the countryside is tough, rural Nicaraguans are generally friendly and cheerful. Despite their hardships, they find ways to get the most enjoyment out of life. On the Caribbean coast, which is sometimes referred to as the Other Nicaragua, life takes on the relaxed pace associated with the Caribbean islands.

Language and Literature

Spanish is the official language of Nicaragua and is spoken by more than 95 percent of the people. The language arrived with Spanish settlers in the 1500s. Since then Nicaraguans have added their own flavor to the language. The result is a vocabulary that mixes in words and phrases from languages spoken by native peoples. Nicaraguans are also known for speaking very rapidly, with words often flowing together.

But Spanish is not the only language spoken in Nicaragua. Native peoples on the Caribbean coast still speak the Miskito, Sumu, and Rama languages. The black residents of the Caribbean coast speak English mixed with languages of African origin—Criollo and Garífuna. In fact, Spanish is seldom heard in some areas of the Caribbean coast.

Poetry is considered one of the most universal art forms in Nicaragua. Former president Daniel Ortega (who wrote a book of poetry) once said, "In Nicaragua, everybody is considered to be a poet until he proves to the contrary." Among the most beloved and

RUBÉN DARÍO

The poet Rubén Darío (1867–1916) is one of Nicaragua's most beloved figures. His face appears on Nicaraguan money, and his name graces bookstores, libraries, and theaters across the nation. His birthplace—the town of San Pedro de Metapa in central Nicaragua—was renamed Ciudad Darío to honor his memory. A diplomat by profession, Darío spent many of his forty-nine years living outside the homeland he celebrated in his verse. But Darío loved his country deeply. He wrote powerfully of his resentment toward the U.S. Marines' occupation of Nicaragua in the early 1900s. In the 1970s, Darío's writing inspired Sandinista leaders. One of Darío"s most-quoted phrases is "If one's nation is small, one makes it large through dreams."

well-known Nicaraguan poets is Rubén Darío (1867–1916). Darío is credited with revolutionizing Latin American literature by using informal language and by experimenting with new literary forms. His influence spread throughout the Spanish-speaking world, and he is praised for adding new vitality to Spanish-language poetry.

Another well-known Nicaraguan poet and author is the Roman Catholic priest Ernesto Cardenal. Cardenal's poetry voices strong criticism of Nicaragua's social injustices under Somoza. After the 1979 revolution, Cardenal became a cultural minister in the Sandinista government. The writing of Gioconda Belli, also a member of the Sandinista movement, captures the spirit of the revolution.

This **public statue of Rubén Darío** is on display in León. Explore www.vgsbooks.com for links to more information about the arts in Nicaragua, its literature, music, dance, theater, and film.

Music

Nicaraguans consider music an important part of their lives, and they play and listen to a variety of styles. Nicaraguan folk music combines elements of indigenous music with European melodies. It features instruments such as the guitar, violin, maracas (bean-filled gourds), and the marimba (a percussion instrument). Nicaraguans are also fans of contemporary popular sounds, including salsa and merengue. These two musical forms combine elements of Caribbean and Spanish music and are popular in many Latin American countries. Ranchera—a Mexican-inspired style of music that features stories of lost love and heartbreak—is common, as well. On the Atlantic coast, Caribbean musical styles such as calypso and reggae can be heard on the streets and in nightclubs.

Film, Theater, and Media

When the Sandinistas came to power in 1979, one of their projects was to create a national film industry. Their efforts resulted in the Nicaraguan Institute of Cinema (INCINE). Young pro-Sandinista film-makers at the institute made fiction and documentary films that promoted the virtues of the Sandinista revolution. The stated goal of INCINE was the "recovery of national identity." INCINE's best-known film was *Alcino and the Condor*, a modern telling of a Latin American folktale about a boy who dreams he can fly. The movie was nominated for an Academy Award for Best Foreign Language Film in 1982. INCINE closed down in 1988 due to lack of funds, and since then there has been little activity in the country's film industry. Most movie theaters in Nicaragua show U.S. films with Spanish subtitles.

Managua is home to most of the country's theatrical venues. Two of these are named after the country's famed poet: El Teatro Nacional Rubén Darío and Teatro Rubén Darío. Both of these theaters host international singing and dancing performances. Sala de Teatro Justo Rufino Garay hosts dance and drama performances by troupes from all over Latin America. Smaller theaters can be found in the cities of Granada and León.

The Nicaraguan press has been a strong force in the country since the days of the Somoza dictatorship. It continues to play an important role in reporting on government corruption. The press vigorously exercises the right to free speech that is protected under the Nicaraguan constitution. Nicaragua's major daily newspapers are *La Prensa* and *El Nuevo Diario*, both published in Managua. They compete with several weekly magazines. The *Tico Times*, published weekly in the Costa Rican capital of San José, is the leading English-language newspaper in Central America.

Internet Servicios is an **Internet café** located in San Juan del Sur.

Although only a small portion of the country's population owns a television set, Nicaragua has seven television stations. These stations carry news programs, Spanish-language soap operas, sporting events, and American shows with Spanish subtitles. Nicaraguans are more likely to be found listening to the country's numerous radio stations. These stations offer traditional music, news, political and economic commentary, and the weekly presidential address.

About 170,000 households in Nicaragua have regular phone service. Cell phones, though still a luxury for many Nicaraguans, are becoming more common. And while less than 10 percent of Nicaraguan households own a personal computer, several Internet service providers operate in the country. For those without computers, cybercafes in Managua and other cities offer access to the Internet. E-mail and chat rooms are becoming popular ways for urban Nicaraguans to communicate with one another and friends in foreign countries.

Art and Architecture

Nicaraguan artisans create a variety of useful craft objects, including pots, baskets, and furniture. Nicaraguan potters produce all sorts of vases, bowls, urns, and pots. Some display the designs of Nicaragua's native peoples. One of the biggest pottery-producing areas is San Juan de Oriente. The town is home to the country's largest pottery cooperative and has been a pottery center since before the arrival of Columbus. The small towns around Masaya have many skilled woodworkers who craft beautiful rocking chairs called *abuelas* (grandmothers). Basket makers throughout the country weave intricate baskets from bamboo, cane, and pine needles.

Nicaragua is also known for its primitivist painting movement. It started on the Solentiname Islands in Lake Nicaragua in the late 1960s. Primitivist paintings reflect the natural beauty of the islands. They often feature brightly colored and highly detailed scenes of peasant life, the lush countryside, and exotic wildlife. Murals (wall paintings) are another popular Nicaraguan art form. During the Sandinista period, murals became a colorful and highly visible form of political protest. Several buildings in León still have murals painted in the 1980s.

Although earthquakes and warfare have done their fare share of damage, Nicaragua still has many buildings from colonial times. For example, colonial-era buildings in Granada and León range from large, ornate churches and government buildings to personal homes. They feature elaborate arched entrances, dramatically carved doorways, and other decorative details. Homes built in the colonial style were usually made of thick stone walls covered in stucco and topped with red tile roofs. Buildings often cluster around large public squares called plazas, as they do in many Spanish towns. Plazas serve as sites for public markets, festivals, and celebrations.

THE ARTISTS OF SOLENTINAME

The primitivist school of painting in Nicaragua began in the late 1960s on the Solentiname Islands. It was founded by Nicaraguan poet and Roman Catholic priest Ernesto Cardenal. Cardenal was on his first trip to the island when he saw a drawing by a local resident and was impressed. Soon Cardenal was giving brushes and paint to other residents and inviting painters to the islands to teach the locals painting techniques. Within a few years, the farmers and fishers of Solentiname were painting scenes of the islands and their daily lives. Although many of Solentiname's painters lack any formal training in art, their colorful depictions of the islands' natural beauty are sold in art galleries around the world.

◐ Religion

The Roman Catholic Church has played an important role in Nicaragua's history—as it has in all Central American countries colonized by Spain. Spanish rulers and early settlers brought the Roman Catholic faith with them to Nicaragua. They converted native peoples to the faith and built churches for worship. As a result, about

73 percent of modern Nicaraguans are Roman Catholic. Churches in urban areas are generally well attended, though attendance is less regular in rural areas. Catholic officials play a very visible role in public life, and their views are widely respected by the public.

Despite the dominance of the Catholic Church, the number of Nicaraguan Protestants (non-Catholic Christians) is about 19 percent. Protestant missionaries (teachers who seek to convert others to their beliefs and churches) have been responsible for this growth. Among the largest of the Protestant faiths is the Moravian Church. It was established by German missionaries on the Caribbean coast in the early 1800s. Many Miskito, Sumu, and Rama Indians belong to the Moravian Church. Many black Nicaraguans belong to the Anglican and Episcopal churches (which were also attended by other English-speaking settlers in the Caribbean Islands). Protestant Nicaraguans also include Baptists, Jehovah's Witnesses, Mormons, and Seventh-day Adventists. Another 8 percent have no religious affiliation. In addition, Nicaragua has small numbers of Jews and Muslims.

Holidays and Festivals

The Nicaraguan year is dotted with religious festivals. Each city and town in Nicaragua has its own patron saint (a Roman Catholic saint considered a protector), and many religious festivals honor familiar saints with parades and other festivities. The patron saint of Managua, Saint Dominic, is honored by the city's residents during the first ten days of August. The Saint Dominic Festival includes religious ceremonies and spectator sports—including horse racing, bullfights, and cockfights. Colorful parades and processions are common during the festival. Holy Week, the week before Easter, is another time of traditional church celebrations. The Thursday and Friday before Easter Sunday (Holy Thursday and Good Friday) are national holidays in Nicaragua. Other religious national holidays include All Souls' Day on November 2 and Christmas on December 25.

El Güegüense is a traditional Nicaraguan folk dance that includes elements of theater. It is often performed at patron saint festivals. Featuring costumed dancers in wooden masks, the dance portrays native Nicaraguans and their reactions to the Spanish conquistadors and their horses.

Nonreligious holidays include Labor Day, held on the first day of May to commemorate the country's workers. On the Caribbean coast, the Palo de Mayo (Maypole) Festival, also held in May, celebrates springtime's arrival.

On May 30, Nicaraguans celebrate Mother's Day. National Liberation Day, which celebrates the victory of the Sandinistas over the Somoza government, is July 19. September 14 marks the anniversary of the Battle of San Jacinto, in which Nicaraguans first defeated the forces of William Walker. September 15 is Independence Day, when Nicaraguans celebrate the freedom won from Spain in 1821.

Sports

Although soccer is a popular sport among Nicaraguans and their Central American neighbors, baseball remains the national game of preference. Nicaraguans young and old play baseball, and almost every town has a baseball diamond. In addition to the many local and youth leagues, Nicaragua has a national baseball league. Made up of six teams, the league plays an eighty-four-game schedule (sixty regular-season games and twenty-four playoff games). Some Nicaraguan players go on to play in the United States, and their compatriots follow their careers avidly. Young people in the cities also play basketball and volleyball.

These **young baseball players** may dream of playing for one of Nicaragua's national baseball league teams. Baseball is the most popular sport in Nicaragua.

It is a fine day for a casual game of soccer on the beach at San Juan del Sur.

Nicaraguans, like other Central Americans, have also become increasingly fond of public parks and recreational facilities. They enjoy camping among their country's beautiful mountains and near the volcanoes.

Nicaragua's coastal waters and lakes attract numerous surfers, windsurfers, sport fishers, and divers from all over the world. In fact, Nicaragua's Pacific coast is considered to have some of the best surfing waves anywhere and is far less crowded than other popular surfing spots. In addition, Nicaragua's volcanic mountains are great for hiking and mountain climbing opportunities.

Food

Most Nicaraguan food includes the staples of rice, beans, and corn. One of the most common Nicaraguan dishes is *gallo pinto* (spotted rooster). This entrée consists of slow-cooked red beans and rice. Corn is typically ground up and made into flat, round tortillas or used for tamales (ground corn wrapped in steamed cornhusks or banana leaves). Another well-known Nicaraguan dish is *nacatamal*, a tamale stuffed with peppers, onions, and pork. Other corn dishes include *atol* (a corn pudding) and *pinol* (a drink made of toasted and ground cornmeal mixed with water, milk, and sometimes chocolate). A typical Nicaraguan meal for any time of the day might include gallo pinto, fried plantains (long, yellow green fruits that resemble bananas), *guajada* (a salty, dry, cheeselike substance), and a corn tortilla.

Meat is a big part of the Nicaraguan diet, though people in rural areas can rarely afford to buy it. Nicaraguan beef, one of the country's biggest exports, is considered to be of exceptional quality. *Bajo* is a traditional Nicaraguan meal consisting of steamed beef served with plantains and yucca, a starchy root vegetable. In Managua and other cities, vendors set up grills on street corners and offer marinated and barbecued beef, chicken, and pork served on tortillas or on squares of banana leaf. On the coasts, fish, shrimp, and lobster are widely available.

GALLO PINTO

This entrée is considered a national dish in Nicaragua. It is often served with tortillas, cheese, and hot sauce, and it is also eaten with eggs as a breakfast dish.

2 c. uncooked white rice

4 c. water

2 tbsp. corn oil

1 medium white onion, chopped

2 15-oz. cans black or red beans, drained

3 tbsp. fresh cilantro, chopped (optional)

2 tsp. salt

1 tsp. black pepper

1. Place rice and 4 c. water in a large pan and bring to a boil over high heat. Reduce heat to medium, cover, and simmer 20 minutes, or until water has been absorbed and rice is tender.
2. Heat oil in a large, deep skillet or stockpot over medium heat. Add onion and sauté 2 to 3 minutes, or until soft but not brown.
3. Add beans and reduce heat to medium low. Stir in half of the cilantro (if using), along with salt and black pepper. Cook, stirring occasionally, for 10 minutes.
4. Add cooked rice to skillet and mix well with beans. Cook 10 minutes longer. Stir in remaining cilantro and serve immediately.

Serves 4 to 6

THE ECONOMY

Nicaragua's economy is still recovering from two damaging forces in the 1980s—warfare and mismanagement. When the Chamorro government took power in 1990, inflation was running at more than 10,000 percent per year, and Nicaraguan currency was nearly worthless. The economy was weak, unemployment was high, and the nation was heavily in debt.

To turn the economy around, the Chamorro government started an economic reform program. The plan included reducing state spending, paying off international debt, and selling state-held industries to private owners. As a result of these measures, inflation slowed by the mid-1990s (dropping from 13,500 percent to below 10 percent). The unemployment rate dropped, as well. The economy slowly began to improve. The United States and other foreign countries started investing in the country. Since then the economy has taken major hits from Hurricane Mitch and from a worldwide drop in coffee prices in 2001. Nevertheless, the Nicaraguan economy continues to improve.

The Nicaraguan economy remains weak, however. The nation is the second-poorest country in the Western Hemisphere after Haiti. In the early 2000s, the country's economy grew by an average of only 2 percent a year, as measured by gross domestic product. (The GDP is the value of all goods and services produced within a country in one year.) Nicaragua still relies heavily on loans from foreign governments and from financial organizations such as the IMF and the World Bank. Unemployment is around 10 percent, while another 40 percent of the population is considered underemployed. The average worker in Nicaragua earns only $750 a year, and more than half the population lives below the poverty line. Nearly 45 percent of the population survives on less than $2 a day. In addition, Nicaragua still has great difficulty in attracting new investment from other countries. And because Nicaragua has a large amount of foreign debt to pay off, it does not have the money to pay for health care, education, and social services for its population.

Agriculture

Agriculture remains the most important sector of the Nicaraguan economy. About 10 percent of Nicaragua's land is used for farming. Agriculture makes up about 30 percent of Nicaragua's GDP and employs nearly 45 percent of the workforce.

Raw coffee beans are Nicaragua's most important export crop. The coffee industry accounts for nearly 19 percent of the country's total agricultural exports and employs nearly 13 percent of the workforce. However, constant changes in world coffee prices mean the amount of money brought in by coffee can differ from year to year. For example, Nicaragua exported $126 million worth of coffee beans in 2004 but only $85 million the previous year. Because of these price changes, Nicaraguan farmers have begun planting other crops, such as peanuts, melons, and onions. Sugarcane, with an annual average of $30 million in export earnings in recent years, is another important export. Rice, corn, and beans are the major food crops grown for use in Nicaragua, followed by bananas, oranges, pineapples, and plantains.

After coffee beans, cattle and cattle products (beef and veal) are the second-largest export items in Nicaragua. Nicaragua's neighbors to the north—Honduras, El Salvador, and Mexico—are big importers of Nicaraguan beef. Dairy products such as milk and cheese are produced mostly for domestic use. In addition to cattle, Nicaraguan farmers also raise pigs, poultry, and horses.

COFFEE TALK

One of the biggest blows to the Nicaraguan economy in recent years was the coffee crisis. This worldwide drop in coffee prices began in 1997 as a result of increased coffee production in the Southeast Asian nation of Vietnam. During the crisis, which ended in 2003, the price of coffee fell to a one-hundred-year low. This severe drop meant many coffee farmers were paying more to produce the coffee than they were earning in return. To revive the coffee industry, Nicaragua is promoting "bird friendly" coffee. Growers want buyers to know that 95 percent of Nicaragua's coffee is grown in forests that also provide a habitat for migrating birds. This "bird friendly" coffee is popular because it is considered less destructive to the environment. In addition, 10 percent of Nicaragua's coffee is grown on small-scale cooperative farms, rather than on large estates. This means it can be marketed as gourmet coffee. For Nicaraguan coffee producers, these labels help ensure more stable prices for their product.

Wild cattle on Ometepe Island in Lake Nicaragua. Some domestic cattle are raised here too, but crops dominate the island's agricultural output. Its volcanic soil is highly fertile.

Another important export item for Nicaragua is seafood. Nicaragua fishers catch and process nearly 30,000 tons (27,216 metric tons) of fish a year. Fishing operations on both coasts net yellowfin tuna, shrimp, and lobster. Shrimp farming is a growing industry in the northwestern section of the country.

Manufacturing

For most of Nicaragua's history, agriculture has far outpaced industry. But that has begun to change, as more countries invest in Nicaraguan industry. Nicaragua has also attracted more companies to the Las Mercedes Industrial Free Trade Zone near Managua. Foreign-owned companies can operate factories in this zone without paying local taxes. The companies that operate in this zone (sixty-five as of 2004) employ more than fifty-eight thousand workers.

Industry accounts for 24 percent of the country's GDP and employs around 17 percent of the workforce. Food processing—the preparation and packaging of meat, vegetables, fruit, fish, and beverages—is one of the biggest industries in Nicaragua. Factories also produce cement, chemicals, machinery, metal products, and wood products. The companies that operate in the free trade zone mostly produce clothing for export to the United States and other countries. Most of Nicaragua's industry is in Managua, where small factories process sugar, meat, cooking oil, and cocoa. Plants in León make leather goods, textiles, and cigars, while factories in Granada process coffee and sugar.

A **horse-drawn taxi** awaits passengers in Managua. Tourists appreciate the horses' slower pace, and taxi owners take pride in keeping their animals and carriages in top condition.

◐ Services and Tourism

Service industries, such as banking, sales, and tourism, account for about 45 percent of Nicaragua's GDP and employ about four out of every ten Nicaraguan workers. Most service jobs are in cities such as Managua, Granada, and León. The majority of the nation's banks, insurance companies, restaurants, hotels, and shopping malls are in these urban areas.

Tourism is the third-largest source of foreign income in Nicaragua. Tourists bring more than $100 million to the Nicaraguan economy each year. For a long time, tourists stayed away from Nicaragua because of its political problems. During those years, the tourism economy was nearly nonexistent. But that began to change in the late 1990s, as the country started to shed its image as a war-torn, politically unstable land. New resorts and hotels sprang up along the Pacific coast. To encourage the growth of the tourism industry, the government provides a ten-year tax break to newly built tourist facilities. Like its neighbor to the south, Costa Rica, Nicaragua has an exotic natural landscape that could be very attractive to ecotourists—travelers who want to observe tropical wildlife in its natural state. Growing tourism in Nicaragua could create a host of travel-related companies and create thousands of new jobs, providing a huge boost to the economy.

Although the tourism industry is rapidly growing, it has a long way to go yet. Many people are still afraid to visit a country with its history of violence. While Costa Rica draws nearly 1 million visitors each year, fewer than 500,000 visit Nicaragua. To attract more tourists and

convince hotel and resort chains that the country is a wise investment, Nicaragua will have to remain politically stable. It will also
have to improve its infrastructure, especially along the hard-to-reach
Caribbean coast.

Energy and Mining

Nicaragua does not contain any large quantities of oil or natural gas. It
must import these items from other nations to meet its energy needs.
In recent years, however, U.S. companies have been exploring the
potential of oil and natural gas deposits off Nicaragua's Pacific and
Carribean coastlines. The nation's major source of fuel remains wood,
which meets half of all its energy demands. The country also operates
two geothermal plants. Geothermal energy uses heated, underground
water sources to generate power. Two hydroelectric plants, powered by
rivers, operate in Nicaragua. The rapid streams of the Central
Highlands have hydroelectric potential but will require large investments before the power can be harnessed.

Mining accounts for less than 1 percent of the nation's GDP.
Nicaragua has small deposits of valuable metals and minerals, including gold, silver, copper, tungsten, lead, and zinc.

Foreign Trade

Foreign trade is a significant part of the Nicaraguan economy. The
country relies on exports to bring in money. Similarly, it depends on
imports to provide many basic foodstuffs and other necessities for its
people. The United States is Nicaragua's main trading partner. It provides more than 25 percent of its imports and receives more than 60
percent of its exports. Nicaragua's principal Latin American trading
partners are Costa Rica, El Salvador, Mexico, Venezuela, Honduras,
and Guatemala. Nicaragua also trades with Canada, Japan, and several
European nations.

Nicaragua's main exports are coffee, beef, gold, seafood, peanuts,
sugar, chemical products, and bananas. Nicaragua imports raw mate-
rials for construction and manufacturing, heavy machinery and equip-
ment, petroleum products, and consumer goods. Overall, the country
has a large trade deficit. This means that the value of its imports is
greater than the value of its exports. On average, the value of the goods
that Nicaragua imports is nearly three times the value of what it
exports. This deficit is one reason that Nicaragua relies so heavily on
foreign aid and loans. However, a free trade zone throughout the
Americas, currently in the planning stages, could boost foreign trade for
Nicaragua and other Central American nations and encourage new
businesses.

Find links to the latest news from Nicaragua, including up-to-date information about its economy, at www.vgsbooks.com.

◉ Transportation

Nicaragua has about 11,800 miles (18,990 km) of roads. Only about 1,240 miles (1,996 km) of these are paved. A system of paved roads links most cities and towns of western and central Nicaragua, but many of those roads are in poor condition. The Pan-American Highway, which travels across many parts of Central and South America, joins several major Nicaraguan cities in the Pacific Lowlands. The highway, which is Nicaragua's best-maintained road, skirts the shore of Lake Nicaragua before crossing the border into Costa Rica. The lowlands of the country's eastern half remain isolated and poorly served by the nation's transportation system. Nearly all the roads in the Caribbean Lowlands are dirt roads that frequently wash out during the long rainy season. The only paved road into eastern Nicaragua ends at the town of Rama. A boat service along the Escondido River links Rama to Bluefields on the Caribbean coast. In some regions of the Caribbean coast, boat travel is the only reliable means of transportation.

Because the majority of the population does not own a car, many Nicaraguans use public buses. The buses link larger towns such as Managua, León, and Chinandega. Crowded and inexpensive buses operate in the capital. In remote villages that have no paved roads, inhabitants use mules and oxcarts to travel and to transport their harvests.

Buses are the most common form of mass transportation. They are usually crowded in Managua and other parts of Nicaragua. Sometimes tourists instead choose to hire a taxi.

Augusto Sandino International Airport in Managua is the country's main hub for air transportation. Two domestic airlines provide service from Managua to Bluefields, the Corn Islands, and other destinations along the Caribbean coast. International carriers link the country to North America, South America, and Europe.

The Future

Although severely damaged by many years of conflict, government mismanagement, and natural disasters, Nicaragua is inching along the path to recovery. The political stability and economic reforms that began in the 1990s have led to better economic performance and increased foreign investment.

But Nicaragua still has a long way to go. It remains a deeply impoverished and indebted country. Despite receiving nearly $4 billion in debt reduction from the IMF, Nicaragua must still make payments on its foreign debt. This steady flow of money out of the country makes new investment in equipment, factories, and social services difficult. To pay off its debts more quickly, Nicaragua needs to promote further economic growth. Attracting more foreign investment is one way to reach this goal.

The Bolaños government is continuing the economic reforms of its predecessors by privatizing more factories and industries. In order to move forward with its plans, the government is trying to gain the cooperation of the country's powerful labor unions. The Bolaños government is also attempting to resolve the long-standing conflict over land seized by the Sandinista government. This issue remains a sore point for many Nicaraguans.

Nicaragua also faces environmental and social challenges. A weak economy and a growing population will continue to put strains on the land. These factors may force poor rural people to clear more of the country's forests for farmland. This deforestation could, in turn, result in more environmental damage and ultimately lead to health problems for the rural population. The nation's leaders must find a way to solve these problems.

Finally, Nicaragua's leaders must find a way to resolve their differences without turning to violence. Although the recent standoff between President Bolaños and the National Assembly has been peaceful, it threatens to damage the democratic process. For Nicaragua to continue on the road to economic improvement, it must remain politically stable—a key factor in attracting tourism dollars and foreign investment. The country's future depends on it.

Timeline

12,000 B.C	Human settlement of Nicaragua begins.
1000 B.C.	Permanent settlements are established in Nicaragua.
A.D 1200	Nicarao and Chorotega peoples migrate into the Pacific Lowlands and Central Highlands from Mexico and Guatemala.
1502	Christopher Columbus explores the Caribbean coasts of present-day Nicaragua, Costa Rica, and Honduras.
1522	Captain Gil González Dávila leads an exploration of Nicaragua's interior.
1524	Francisco Hernández de Córdoba establishes the cities of León and Granada.
1543	Captaincy General of Guatemala is founded. Nicaragua becomes part of this political unit.
1610	Momotombo Volcano erupts, destroying León. The Spanish settlers relocate the city to its present location.
1821	The nations of Central America declare themselves independent of Spain.
1823	Nicaragua, Costa Rica, Honduras, El Salvador, and Guatemala establish the United Provinces of Central America.
1838	The United Provinces of Central America is dissolved.
1855	U.S. soldier William Walker and an army of supporters overthrow the government of Nicaragua.
1856	Walker holds a rigged election and declares himself president.
1857	Walker surrenders in the town of Rivas and is sent back to the United States.
1858	Managua becomes the capital of Nicaragua.
1876	Telegraph service begins in Nicaragua.
1909	U.S. Marines help Conservative politicians overthrow Liberal president José Santos Zelaya.
1916	Nicaragua and the United States sign the Chamorro-Bryan Treaty. It gives the United States a claim to any future canal route by way of the San Juan River.
1927	Liberals and Conservatives agree to the U.S.-sponsored Espino Negro Pact. Augusto Sandino refuses to accept the agreement and begins his guerrilla campaign against the government and U.S. forces.
1933	U.S. Marines withdraw from Nicaragua.
1934	Officers of the Guardia Nacional arrest and execute Sandino.

1937 General Anastasio Somoza García is elected president.

1956 Anastasio Somoza is assassinated. His son Luis becomes interim president.

1963 Luis Somoza's handpicked successor, René Schick, is elected president.

1967 Tachito Somoza, chief of the Guardia Nacional, wins the presidential election.

1972 An earthquake of 6.3 on the Richter scale devastates Managua.

1976 Nicaraguan Dennis Martinez makes his U.S. Major League Baseball debut with the Baltimore Orioles.

1979 Tachito Somoza flees the country, and the Sandinistas take over the Nicaraguan government.

1982 The Nicaraguan film *Alcino and the Condor* is nominated for an Academy Award for Best Foreign Language Film.

1984 In the midst of a growing conflict between the Sandinista government and Contra forces, Sandinista candidate Daniel Ortega Saavedra wins the presidential election.

1985 The United States halts all trade with Nicaragua.

1987 Costa Rican president Oscar Arias Sánchez puts forth a peace plan to end the fighting in Nicaragua.

1988 The Sandinista government agrees to a cease-fire with the Contras.

1990 Violeta Chamorro defeats Daniel Ortega in the presidential election.

1998 Hurricane Mitch devastates Nicaragua, killing thousands and leaving many more homeless.

2004 After several years of negotiations with the United States and Central American nations, the Nicaraguan government signs the Dominican Republic-Central America Free Trade Agreement.

2005 President Enrique Bolaños and the National Assembly agree to postpone constitutional reforms until 2007.

COUNTRY NAME Republic of Nicaragua

AREA 50,193 square miles (130,000 sq. km)

MAIN LANDFORMS Caribbean Lowlands, Central Highlands, Pacific Lowlands, Chontalena range, Isabella range, Dariense range, Ometepe Island, Corn Islands, Cosigüina Volcano, Masaya Volcano, Mombacho Volcano, Momotombo Volcano, San Cristóbal Volcano, Telica Volcano

HIGHEST POINT Mount Mogoton, 8,000 feet (2,438 m) above sea level

LOWEST POINT Sea level

MAJOR RIVERS Coco, Escondido, San Juan, Matagalpa

ANIMALS Anteaters, armadillos, boa constrictors, crocodiles, deer, falcons, hawks, herons, jaguars, manatees, monkeys, ocelots, ospreys, peccaries, pelicans, pumas, sea turtles, tapirs

CAPITAL CITY Managua

OTHER MAJOR CITIES León, Chinandega, Masaya, Granada, Estelí

OFFICIAL LANGUAGE Spanish

MONETARY UNIT Cordoba. 100 centavos = 1 cordoba.

NICARAGUA'S CURRENCY

The currency of Nicaragua is known as the cordoba. It is named after Francisco Hernández de Córdoba, who established the first Spanish settlement in Nicaragua. Each cordoba is divided into 100 centavos. Nicaragua issues bills (paper money) in denominations of 2, 5, 10, 20, 50, 100, 200, 500, 1,000, 5,000, and 10,000 cordobas and coins worth 1, 2, 5, and 10 cordobas. About 16 cordobas equal one U.S. dollar.

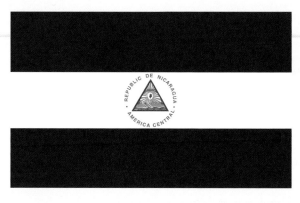

The Nicaraguan flag was adopted in 1971. It displays three horizontal bands. From top to bottom, the bands are blue, white, and blue. The two blue stripes stand for the Pacific Ocean and the Caribbean Sea, as well as justice and loyalty. The white stripe represents peace, virtue, and purity. At the center of the flag, inside the center of the white stripe, is the country's coat of arms. This symbol features a triangle encircled by the words *REPUBLIC DE NICARAGUA* on the top and *AMERICA CENTRAL* on the bottom. Inside the triangle, five volcanoes rise up from the water. The five volcanoes represent the five nations of the former United Provinces of Central America—Nicaragua, Costa Rica, Honduras, Guatemala, and El Salvador.

Flag

Nicaragua's national anthem is "Salve a ti, Nicaragua" (Hail to Thee, Nicaragua). The music is based on a religious hymn brought to Nicaragua by a Spanish monk in the 1700s. It was arranged by Spanish composer Luis Abraham Delgadillo. In 1918 the government held a contest to search for new words to the music. Salomon Ibarra Mayorga, a teacher and poet, was the winner of the contest. Here are two verses from the national anthem in English:

National Anthem

Hail to Thee, Nicaragua
Hail to thee, Nicaragua!
The voice of the cannon no longer roars on your soil,
Nor does the blood of brothers stain
Your glorious bicolor flag.

Peace shines beautiful in your sky,
Nothing dims your immortal glory,
For work is what earns your laurels
And honor is your triumphal ensign!

 Discover what the melody of Nicaragua's national anthem, "Salve a ti, Nicaragua," sounds like. Go to www.vgsbooks.com for a link.

GIOCONDA BELLI (b. 1948) One of Nicaragua's best-known living writers, Belli was born in Managua. In the 1970s, she became a member of the Sandinista movement and worked to overthrow the Somoza government. Her most famous book is *The Inhabited Woman*. It tells the story of a privileged woman who takes part in a movement to overthrow the dictator of an imaginary Latin American country. The story is loosely based on her life.

ERNESTO CARDENAL (b. 1925) Born in Granada, Cardenal is a poet, a Roman Catholic priest, and a central figure in the Sandinista movement. Cardenal served as Nicaragua's minister of culture from 1979 to 1987. He is also credited as the founder of the primitivist painting movement on the Solentiname Islands.

VIOLETA BARRIOS DE CHAMORRO (b. 1929) Born in the town of Rivas, Chamorro became the editor of the anti-Somoza newspaper *La Prensa* after her husband, Pedro Chamorro, was assassinated by members of the Guardia Nacional. Chamorro was a member of the Sandinista government until 1980, when she resigned in protest against Sandinista power. Chamorro defeated Daniel Ortega in the 1990 presidential election and served as president until 1996.

RUBÉN DARÍO (1867–1916) Born in the town of San Pedro de Metapa, Darío went on to become Nicaragua's most important artistic figure. Darío is considered the father of the modernist movement in Latin America. Modernism was an artistic movement that aimed to reinvent traditional forms of art and literature. His unique writing style is credited with revolutionizing Latin American literature. In addition to being a journalist and a poet, Darío was a diplomat who served as Nicaragua's ambassador to Spain.

CARLOS FONSECA (1936–1976) Born in Matagalpa, Fonseca was involved with political groups as a teenager before becoming the founding member of the Sandinista National Liberation Front. Fonseca was assassinated by members of the Guardia Nacional in 1976 and is considered one of the major figures of the Sandinista revolution.

BIANCA JAGGER (b. 1945) A prominent social and political activist, Bianca Jagger was born in Managua. She became involved in issues of justice and human rights after returning to Nicaragua in 1979 and witnessing the brutality of the Somoza regime. In the 1980s, she was a supporter of the Sandinista government and fought to raise awareness of the U.S. government's involvement in the Nicaraguan civil war. She is active in several human rights groups and has won many awards for her work.

DENNIS MARTÍNEZ (b. 1955) Born in Granada, Martínez went on to become the first baseball player from Nicaragua to play in Major League Baseball. A right-handed pitcher known by the nickname *El Presidente (The President)*, Martínez posted 245 victories over a twenty-three-year career (the most wins of any Latin American pitcher in the Major Leagues). The baseball park in Managua is named after him.

DANIEL ORTEGA SAAVEDRA (b. 1945) Born in the village of La Libertad, Ortega joined the Sandinista movement as a teenager and eventually became its most public face. After spending several years in prison for his political activity, Ortega became a member of the junta that governed Nicaragua after the victory over Somoza. He served as president of Nicaragua from 1985 to 1990. Although he was defeated in presidential elections in 1996 and 2001, Ortega remains a powerful figure in Nicaraguan politics.

AUGUSTO CÉSAR SANDINO (1895–1934) Born in the village of Niquinohomo to a prominent coffee grower, Sandino became a symbol of Nicaraguan resistance to U.S. occupation. From 1926 to 1933, Sandino led a guerrilla movement against the government and U.S. forces. During this time, he developed tactics and strategies of guerrilla warfare that have since been used effectively by rebel movements in all parts of the world. He also fought to defend exploited workers and landless peasants. His actions led a later revolutionary movement, the Sandinistas, to name their group after him.

ANASTASIO SOMOZA GARCÍA (1896–1956) Born in San Marcos, Somoza was Nicaragua's leader from 1937 to 1956 and the head of a dynasty that ruled the country for more than forty years. Somoza was schooled in the United States. He also worked in the automobile business in Philadelphia, Pennsylvania. These experiences provided him with two assets of great value in his rise to power—the ability to converse easily in the English language and an understanding of U.S. politics and culture. Somoza was assassinated in 1956. He was succeeded as president by his two sons, Luis Somoza Debayle and Anastasio Somoza Debayle.

INDIO MAÍZ BIOLOGICAL RESERVE This reserve, bordering the San Juan River in southeastern Nicaragua, is dedicated to the preservation of plant and animal species in their natural ecosystem. It is one of the few areas remaining in the Americas where visitors can experience untouched tropical rain forest.

LA FLOR WILDLIFE RESERVE This beach on Nicaragua's southern Pacific coast plays host every June and July to thousands of paslama turtles, who beach themselves to nest and lay their eggs. Located at the edge of a strip of tropical dry forest, the beach is also home to monkeys, coyotes, and several species of birds.

LEÓN This city in northwestern Nicaragua is one of the best places to get a glimpse of Nicaragua's colonial past. Several churches in the city date back to the 1700s. The Catedral de León (Cathedral of León), built in 1747, is Central America's largest.

MANAGUA As the lively and chaotic capital city of Nicaragua, Managua offers visitors many activities. They can see performances of dance, theater, and music at the Teatro Rubén Darío (the Rubén Darío Theater) or learn about Nicaragua's history and culture at the Palacio Nacional de Culture (the National Palace of Culture—home to Nicaragua's National Library, National Museum, and Institute of Culture). Managua also has several restaurants, nightclubs, and casinos. Fans of baseball can catch a game at the Dennis Martínez Baseball Stadium.

MASAYA VOLCANO NATIONAL PARK This park is in the Pacific Lowlands region of Nicaragua, just north of Lake Nicaragua. It is the most easily accessed volcano in Nicaragua, with a paved road leading right to the crater, an interpretive center, and more than 12 miles (19 km) of trails. The volcano consists of three craters. One contains a visible pool of liquid lava at its center.

MOMBACHO VOLCANO Just outside of Granada, the dormant Mombacho Volcano is home to a spectacular cloud forest. Trails allow visitors to walk through the misty forests and view several species of butterflies and salamanders found only in Nicaragua.

ZAPATERA ARCHIPELAGO NATIONAL PARK This park, in the northwest corner of Lake Nicaragua, consists of the Zapatera Volcano and eight small islands that surround it. The islands still contain virgin forest and are home to statues from Nicaragua's pre-Columbian past.

archaeologist: a scholar who studies the remains of past human cultures

canopy: a top layer of tree leaves and branches that creates a covering over the forest plants below

cloud forests: high-altitude rain forests covered in clouds year-round

colony: a community of immigrants who settle a new land but still follow the laws and government of their homeland

dictatorship: rule by a single person, who usually does not allow dissent or opposition

ecosystem: an interdependent community of plants and animals

encomienda: a rural estate granted to a Spanish colonist. The colonist was also given the right to use the labor of local indigenous people and was expected to oversee their conversion to Christianity.

erosion: the wearing away of soil or rock by wind, rain, ice, or flowing water

free trade zone: areas where businesses can operate without paying local taxes. Free trade zones encourage foreign trade.

gross domestic product (GDP): a measure of the total value of goods and services produced within a country during a certain amount of time (usually one year)

guerrilla: a person who engages in radical and irregular warfare, especially as part of a rebel group

habitat: the natural home of a plant or animal

inflation: a decrease in the value of money, which leads to higher prices

junta: a council, usually consisting of military officials, that rules a country after the government has been overthrown

mestizo: a person of mixed Indian and European ancestry

nationalize: to make assets—businesses, natural resources, or land—the property of government

patron saint: among Catholics, a historical figure sainted by the church and believed to protect a family or community from disease and misfortune

privatize: to sell state-owned assets, such as banks and businesses, to private owners and foreign investors

rain forest: a complex ecosystem of trees, plants, and animals that thrive in humidity and heavy rainfall

Selected Bibliography

Belli, Gioconda. *The Country Under My Skin: A Memoir of Love and War.* **New York: Anchor Books, 2003.**
This memoir by a former member of the Sandinistas provides an inside account of the oppressive Somoza regime and the revolution that brought the Sandinistas to power.

Berman, Joshua, and Randy Wood. *Moon Handbooks Nicaragua.* **Emeryville, CA: Avalon Travel Publishing, 2003.**
This detailed travel guide offers great insight into the history, culture, politics, and economics of Nicaragua. The authors are two former Peace Corps members who lived and worked in Nicaragua.

Dematteis, Lou, and Chris Vail, eds. *Nicaragua: A Decade of Revolution.* **New York: W. W. Norton, 1991.**
A photographic chronology of the years 1979 to 1990, this book depicts the Sandinista revolution, the civil war against the Contras, and the presidential race between Daniel Ortega and Violeta Chamorro.

Diederich, Bernard. *Somoza and the Legacy of U.S. Involvement in Central America.* **New York: E. P. Dutton, 1981.**
This history of the Somoza dynasty emphasizes Tachito Somoza and the revolution that deposed him as Nicaragua's ruler.

Heyck, Denis Lynn Daly. *Life Stories of the Nicaraguan Revolution.* **New York: Routledge, 1990.**
In this collection of interviews, more than twenty Nicaraguans—politicians, priests, farmers, doctors, and teachers—talk about their experiences during the Sandinista revolution. It provides a look at how Nicaragua's conflicts affected peoples' lives.

Miranda, Roger, and William Ratcliff. *The Civil War in Nicaragua: Inside the Sandinistas.* **New Brunswick, NJ: Transactional Publishers, 1994.**
The authors of this book are a member of the Sandinista government and a Stanford University professor. They describe the failures of the Sandinista leadership and discuss how the Sandinista revolution failed to help improve the lot of the Nicaraguan people.

Rushdie, Salman. *The Jaguar Smile: A Nicaraguan Journey.* **New York: Picador USA, 2003.**
This portrait of the people, land, politics, and poetry of Nicaragua is assembled from interviews with Sandinista politicians, poor farmers, and soldiers during the civil war of the 1980s.

Walker, Thomas W. *Nicaragua: The Land of Sandino.* **Boulder, CO: Westview Press, 1991.**
This review of Nicaragua's history focuses on the conflict between the Sandinistas and the Contras.

White, Randy Wayne. *The Sharks of Lake Nicaragua: True Tales of Adventure, Travel, and Fishing.* Guilford, CT: The Lyons Press, 2000.
The title piece of this collection of essays details the author's search for the fabled freshwater sharks of Lake Nicaragua and provides a portrait of Nicaragua's landscape and people.

Woodward, Ralph Lee, Jr. *Central America: A Nation Divided.* New York: Oxford University Press, 1999.
A survey of the Central American region, this book covers the history of Nicaragua, Guatemala, Belize, Honduras, Costa Rica, El Salvador, and Panama from pre-Columbian times to the present.

Behnke, Alison. *Cooking the Central American Way.* **Minneapolis: Lerner Publications Company, 2005.**
This cookbook provides culturally authentic recipes from Nicaragua and its neighboring countries. It also offers the history and cultural traditions associated with these dishes.

Cockroft, James. *Daniel Ortega.* **New York: Chelsea House, 1991.**
This book for young readers is a biography of the former Nicaraguan president that also traces the rise of the Sandinista movement and the overthrow of the Somoza regime.

Gelman, Rita Goldman. *Inside Nicaragua: Young People's Dreams and Fears.* **New York: Franklin Watts, 1988.**
Through interviews with young people throughout Nicaragua, the author describes how the lives of Nicaragua's youth have been affected by the conflict between the Sandinistas and the Contras.

Lindop, Laurie. *Probing Volcanoes.* **Minneapolis: Twenty-First Century Books, 2003.**
This book explores the science of volcanoes and presents a rare behind-the-scenes look at the extreme risks scientists take in the field.

Malone, Michael R. *A Nicaraguan Family.* **Minneapolis: Lerner Publications Company, 1998.**
A Nicaraguan family in the United States describes their flight from Managua in 1979 to a new life in Miami.

Nicaragua, a Country with a Heart
http://www.intur.gob.ni/index_eng.html
This site, operated by the Nicaraguan Institute of Tourism, offers information on travel destinations in Nicaragua.

Resource Center of the Americas.org
http://www.americas.org
This website provides links to newspapers and magazines with up-to-date information about events in Nicaragua.

Rohmer, Harriet, Virginia Stearns, and Dorminster Wilson. *Mother Scorpion Country.* **San Francisco: Children's Book Press, 1987.**
This illustrated book for young readers is a bilingual (English-Spanish) retelling of a Miskito Indian myth.

Streissguth, Tom. *Costa Rica in Pictures.* **Minneapolis: Twenty-First Century Books, 2005.**
Nicaragua has a lot in common with Costa Rica, its neighbor to the south. This book examines Costa Rica's geography, history, government, peoples, cultural life, and economy.

Further Reading and Websites

Tico Times Online Edition
http://www.ticotimes.net/

Billing itself as the leading daily English newspaper of Central America, the *Tico Times* posts this website with business and tourism information, listings of cultural events, and news reports.

vgsbooks.com
http://www.vgsbooks.com

Visit vgsbooks.com, the homepage of the Visual Geography Series®. You can get linked to all sorts of useful on-line information, including geographical, historical, demographic, cultural, and economic websites. The vgsbooks.com site is a great resource for late-breaking news and statistics.

Woods, Michael, and Mary B. Woods. *Volcanoes.* Minneapolis: Lerner Publications Company, 2007.

This books explores the science of volcanoes and presents a close-up look at the impact active volcanoes have on people and their communities.

Young, Alan M., and Judith Huf. *Tropical Rainforests.* New York: St. Martin's Press, 2001.

This book for young readers provides detailed descriptions and illustrations of the various plants, insects, reptiles, birds, and mammals that live in rain forests in Nicaragua and elsewhere.

Captions for photos appearing on cover and chapter openers:

Cover: Volcano Concepción appears in the distance beyond a coffee co-operative in Balgue.

pp. 4–5 Lake Managua shimmers on the horizon of this birds-eye view of Nicaragua's capital city, Managua.

pp. 8–9 Near Granada the cone of Volcano Masaya *(left)* contrasts with the flat, fertile lands beyond it *(right)*. Masaya is the most continually active volcano in Nicaragua.

pp. 42–43 People await buses at a depot in Masaya.

pp. 48–49 Sculptures displayed on the Republic Plaza in Managua depict Spaniards arriving in the 1500s.

Photo Acknowledgments
The images in this book are used with the permission of: © Joshua Sjogren, pp. 4–5, 11, 18, 22, 45, 48–49, 50, 52, 56, 62; © XNR Productions, pp. 6, 12; © Grant Fleming/Art Directors, pp. 8–9, 36; © Edward Parker/Art Directors, p. 13; © Cory Langley, pp. 15, 42–43, 44, 55, 61, 64; © Reuters/CORBIS, p. 16; Library of Congress, pp. 25 (LC-USZ62-8623), 27 (LC-USZ62-108152); © Bettmann/CORBIS, p. 29; © Thomas D. Mcavoy/Time Life Pictures/Getty Images, p. 31; Earth Science Photographic Archive, U.S. Geological Survey Photo Library (USGS), p. 33; © Matthew Naythons/Liaison/Getty Images, p. 34; © Arthur Robles/Time Life Pictures/Getty Images, p. 38; © Sam Lund/Independent Picture Service, p. 68; Laura Westlund, p. 69.

Front Cover: © Margie Politzer/Lonely Planet Images; Back Cover: © NASA.